THE COMPLETE CARB-CYCLING COOKBOOK FOR BEGINNERS

A Comprehensive Guide to Carb Cycling with Easy-to-Follow Steps for High-Carb and Low-Carb Days, with Quick and Easy Recipes to Maximize Your Weight Loss

By Eloise Hewitt

TABLE OF CONTENT

INTRODUCTION

The carb-cycling diet is a popular weight-loss method that has gained significant attention recently. It is a flexible diet that alternates between high- carbohydrate and low-carbohydrate days to improve metabolism, enhance energy levels, and promote fat loss.

The concept behind the carb-cycling diet is simple. By alternating between high-carbohydrate and low-carbohydrate days, the body is forced to adapt to macronutrient changes, stimulating metabolism and promoting fat loss. On high-carbohydrate days, the diet emphasizes consuming complex carbohydrates like whole grains, fruits, and vegetables, while on low-carbohydrate days, the diet focuses on high protein and fat intake.

The carb-cycling diet has gained popularity because of its flexibility, allowing individuals to customize it to their preferences and lifestyle. For instance, athletes and bodybuilders may opt for a more aggressive carb-cycling plan, while those seeking a more gradual weight loss may opt for a less intense schedule.

One of the significant benefits of the carb-cycling diet is its ability to improve insulin sensitivity. Insulin is a hormone that regulates blood sugar levels, and its overproduction can lead to weight gain and metabolic disorders like diabetes. By cycling carbohydrates, the body can better regulate insulin production, reducing the risk of insulin resistance and diabetes.

Another benefit of the carb-cycling diet is its ability to preserve muscle mass while promoting fat loss. By consuming high protein on low-carbohydrate days, the body is supplied with enough amino acids to support muscle growth and repair, even during periods of calorie restriction. This is crucial for athletes and bodybuilders who want to reduce their body fat percentage while maintaining lean muscle mass.

The carb-cycling diet is a flexible, effective, and sustainable weight-loss method that has recently gained significant popularity. Its ability to improve insulin sensitivity, preserve muscle mass, and promote fat loss makes it attractive for anyone looking to lose weight and improve their overall health. However, like any diet, it is essential to consult a healthcare professional before starting the carb- cycling diet to ensure it is safe and appropriate for your individual needs.

CHAPTER 1: THE BASICS OF THE CARB-CYCLING DIET

The primary component of the carb cycling regimen is eating more or fewer carbohydrates on alternate days. Among other benefits, carb cycling may help people manage the symptoms of long-term chronic conditions, lose weight, and enhance their athletic ability. Although much of the weight you might lose is likely water, this method is increasingly popular with people who want to accelerate weight reduction.

You usually eat more carbohydrates when you plan to do vigorous exercise. On those days, you typically consume 2 to 2.5 grams of carbohydrates for every pound of your body weight since your body requires additional nourishment. You eat fewer carbohydrates on days when you're not occupied, busy, or physically active. Therefore, on low-carb days you should consume 0.5 grams of carbohydrates for every pound of body weight. Moreover, consuming no more than 30 grams of carbohydrates on a no-carb day would be best.

Daily Carbohydrate amounts on Carb Cycling:

A. Low Carb: Less than 26% of a person's daily calories should be from carbohydrates.
B. Moderate Carb: Individuals consume 26-44% of their daily calories from carbohydrates.
C. High Carb: A person's daily calorie intake consists of at least 45% carbohydrates.

Carb cycling's fundamental tenet is adjusting your carb intake by changing requirements over a week, month, or year. Each phase has a different timing and carbohydrate intake based on the individual.

Carb cycling was first widely used by bodybuilders and high-performing athletes, but it is now more frequently used by recreational athletes and individuals who want to lose weight. Carb cycling typically centers around a person's training regimen. Athletes would choose high-carb days when training more rigorously and low-carb days when training less rigorously. This alternating between days with high carbs and days with reduced carbs is essentially the basic principle of Carb-cycling. Even "no-carb" days could occur.

There are two main purposes or benefits of Carb-Cycling:

1. Ensure Peak Performance: Cutting back on carbs before your primary training season starts may help your body better utilize them when you reintroduce them before you need to reach your peak performance level. This benefits those concentrating on endurance sports like running, cycling, and swimming.

2. Weight Loss: A lower-carbohydrate diet may help with weight management, weight loss, and reaching optimal health. Low-carb diets reduce power output during high-intensity exercise, so carb cycling may be helpful if you want to finish an activity but are on a low-carb diet.

CHAPTER 2: THE SCIENCE BEHIND THE CARB-CYCLING DIET

The carb-cycling diet is a diet that has recently gained traction among athletes, bodybuilders, and fitness fanatics. It requires alternating between periods of high and low carbohydrate consumption. This diet encourages muscle gain and fat loss while maximizing the body's usage of carbs for energy. The science behind the carb-cycling diet is based on the principles of nutrient timing and manipulating insulin levels. Carbohydrates, both simple and complex, are the primary fuel source for the human body. These are converted into glucose, which the body uses to power its metabolic functions. However, excess carbohydrate intake can lead to fat storage, contributing to weight gain and obesity. This is where the carb-cycling diet comes in. By alternating between high-carbohydrate and low-carbohydrate days, the body can use carbohydrates more efficiently for energy while promoting fat loss.

The high-carbohydrate days of the carb cycling diet give the body the power to fuel intense workouts and encourage muscle growth. These days, the body's insulin levels are elevated, which promotes glucose uptake by muscle cells. Increased glycogen storage results from this, giving the body a ready supply of energy during exercise. High-carbohydrate days are typically followed by low-carbohydrate days, during which the body's insulin levels are lower. This promotes the breakdown of fat for energy, which can lead to fat loss, and this is the carb-cycling diet's primary strategy for controlling insulin levels.

In our body, insulin, a hormone, regulates how much glucose the body uses. When insulin levels are high, the body is in an anabolic state, which means it can build muscle and store glycogen. When insulin levels are low, the body is in a catabolic state, which means it breaks down fat for energy. The carb-cycling diet may regulate insulin levels to stimulate muscle development and fat reduction by alternating between high-carbohydrate and low-carbohydrate days.

The carb-cycling diet also takes into account the concept of nutrient timing. The timing of food intake during the activity is referred to as "nutrient timing." During the high-carbohydrate days of the carb cycling diet, carbohydrates are consumed before and after workouts to provide the body with the energy it needs to fuel intense exercise and promote muscle growth. On low-carbohydrate days, the emphasis is on protein and fat intake, which can help to promote satiety and prevent muscle breakdown.

The carb-cycling diet has been studied in several clinical trials, and the results have been promising. According to a study published in the Journal of the International Association of Sports Nutrition, overweight women's body composition and fat reduction who followed a carb-cycling diet significantly improved significantly. Another study published in the Journal of the American College of Nutrition found that a carb-cycling diet effectively promoted muscle growth and improved athletic performance in male bodybuilders.

Despite the promising results of these studies, it is essential to note that the carb-cycling diet may only be suitable for some. Before beginning a carb-cycling diet, those with specific medical issues, such as diabetes, should speak with a healthcare provider. Additionally, the carb-cycling diet may not be sustainable in the long term, as it can be challenging to adhere to a strict dietary regimen over an extended period. In conclusion, the science behind the carb-cycling diet is based on the principles of nutrient timing and manipulating insulin levels. By alternating between periods of high-carbohydrate and low-carbohydrate intake, the body can use carbohydrates more efficiently for energy while promoting fat loss and muscle growth. Although the carb-cycling diet is not for everyone, it has shown potential in clinical trials.

In theory, carb-cycling might make logic, but what does the scientific community think of it? The biological mechanisms underlying carbohydrate regulation are the cornerstone of the science of carb cycling. The goal of carb cycling is to provide your body with the calories or carbohydrates it needs. For example, it provides carbohydrates before or following vigorous exercise practice. On days when you consume a lot of carbohydrates, your body refills its stores of muscle glycogen, potentially improving performance and reducing muscle breakdown.

Scientific experts have also shown that leptin and ghrelin's capacity to regulate appetite and weight may also be strengthened by strategically scheduled high-carb periods. During the low-carb days, your body switches to a fat-based energy system, which may improve metabolic flexibility and your body's capability to burn fat as fuel in the long run.

It's also crucial to remember that controlling insulin is a crucial aspect of glucose cycling. Utilizing low-carb days and planning carbohydrate intake to coincide with physical exercise may enhance insulin sensitivity and reduce the risk of contracting a variety of diseases, including diabetes. Looking to increase your insulin sensitivity is a smart and healthy decision whether you have diabetes or not.

Two categories of carbs exist Simple and complex carbohydrates. While complex carbohydrates have three or more sugar units, simple carbohydrates only have one or two. Starches like those found in grains, beans, and potatoes are examples of complex carbohydrates.

For your body to function properly, you need carbohydrates. Your body obtains its energy from carbohydrates, proteins, and lipids. However, compared to fat, which has 9 calories per gram, protein, and carbohydrates only have 4. Approximately 50% to 55% of your daily calories should come from carbohydrates, 10% to 15% from proteins, and less than 30% from lipids, according to specialists.

Carbs come in a variety of healthful forms. Natural sources of Carbs include dairy products and foods made from plants, such as grains, fruits, veggies, beans, and fruits. Carbohydrates are broken down into glucose during digestion, which your body utilizes as fuel. You may experience fewer carb cravings and more energy once you cease using carbohydrates as a source of energy.

Refined carbohydrates and simple sugars, which are found in baked goods, highly processed snacks, and cakes, should only be eaten in moderation in carb-cycling. When planning your high-carb days, take into account these healthier food choices:

a) **Whole grains:** Unaltered or unprocessed grains like brown rice, grains, and quinoa may offer several health advantages in the carb-cycling diet. Reduce your consumption of processed meals, refined carbohydrates, and added sugars.
b) **Vegetables:** Each veggie has a unique vitamin and mineral makeup. To obtain a balanced diet in carb-cycling, consume a variety of colors.
c) **Whole fruits:** Choose high-fiber fruits and vegetables.
d) **Legumes:** These are excellent choices for fiber- and mineral-rich, slowly digesting carbs.
e) **Tubers:** This includes potatoes and sweet potatoes.
f) **Dairy:** Pick low-fat varieties of milk, cheese, yogurt, and other dairy goods when you are in carb-cycling.

What to eat on high and low-carb days can be tailored to an individual's dietary preferences and nutritional needs.

On high- carbohydrate days, the emphasis is on consuming complex carbohydrates that are high in fiber and provide a sustained release of energy throughout the day. High-carbohydrate foods include whole grains, such as brown rice, quinoa, and whole wheat pasta; fruits, such as bananas, apples, and berries; and vegetables, such as sweet potatoes, corn, and peas. These foods are also high in antioxidants, minerals, and vitamins that help with general health and well-being. In addition to complex carbohydrates, it is important to consume lean protein sources, such as chicken, turkey, fish, and low-fat dairy products, to support muscle recovery and growth. Healthy fats, such as nuts, seeds, and avocado, can also be included in moderation to provide additional energy and promote satiety.

On low-carbohydrate days, the emphasis is on consuming protein-rich foods and healthy fats to promote fat loss and prevent muscle breakdown. Lean meats, such as fish, turkey, and chicken; eggs; and plant-based protein sources, such as tempeh, tofu, and legumes, are protein-rich. Good fats, such as avocado, olive oil, nuts, and seeds, give long-lasting energy and help you feel full. During low-carbohydrate days, it is critical to restrict or eliminate high-carbohydrate items such as bread, spaghetti, and sugary snacks.

To ensure optimal nutrition and meet individual dietary needs, it is important to include a variety of foods in both high-carbohydrate and low-carbohydrate meals. This can be achieved by incorporating different fruits, vegetables, whole grains, and protein sources into weekly meals. It is also important to remain hydrated by drinking lots of water and other low-calorie liquids like herbal tea and flavored water.

While the carb-cycling diet can effectively promote fat loss and muscle growth, it is important to note that it may not suit everyone. Before beginning a carb-cycling diet, anyone with specific medical issues, such as diabetes, should speak with a healthcare expert. Additionally, the carb-cycling diet may not be sustainable in the long term, as it can be difficult to adhere to a strict dietary regimen over an extended period. It is important to find a nutritional approach that is enjoyable, sustainable, and meets individual dietary needs for optimal health and well-being.

Recommended Carbs

All protein and fats such as:
- Beef
- Eggs
- Bacon
- Macadamia Nuts
- Pistachios
- Chicken
- Pork
- Salmon
- Tuna
- Shrimp
- Avocado
- Olive Oil
- Mackerel
- Coconut Oil
- Butter
- Almonds
- Cashews

Carbs To Avoid Or Limit

- Ice Cream
- Russet potatoes
- Any fruits outside of blueberries or strawberries
- Bread
- Sugary drinks
- Pastas
- Sweet potatoes
- Candy

CHAPTER 4: WEIGHT LOSS EXERCISES ON CARB-CYCLING DIET

Bodybuilders and athletes have long used a classic strategy to help them get the most out of their nutrition and training: training hard on some days and light on others. It's common to want to plan your nutrition around your workouts if you're carb cycling. Therefore, it makes sense to match your nutrition with your most difficult and straightforward exercises if you carb cycle. When you consume more carbs on a day when you work out hard, such as a lower-body workout or a challenging circuit workout, you are balancing your diet. The smaller muscle workouts like those for the arms, shoulders, and abs, the lower-intensity cardio, or a rest day would be done on the lower-carb days. Here is an easy illustration of a workout schedule that isn't too drawn out and strenuous:

DAY	CARB-CYCLE	CARBS	EXERCISE
Monday	High-Carb	200 g	Weight Training
Tuesday	Moderate-Carb	100 g	Aerobic Exercise
Wednesday	Low-Carb	30 g	Rest Day
Thursday	High-Carb	200 g	Weight Training
Friday	High-Carb	200 g	Weight Training
Saturday	Low-Carb	30 g	Rest Day
Sunday	Low-Carb	30 g	Rest Day

WEEK 1

DAY	CARB INTAKE	BREAKFAST	SNACK	LUNCH	SNACK	DINNER	TOTAL CARBS
Monday	High Carb	Pumpkin waffles	Tofu and vegetable skewers	Black Pepper Salmon with yogurt	Pizza Breadsticks	High-Carb Farfalle Pasta with Mushrooms	220g
Tuesday	Moderate Carb	Apple omelet	Thai Tempeh cabbage leaf rolls	Caprese Pesto Chicken	Pizza Breadsticks	Stewed Cashew Vegetables	140g
Wednesday	Low Carb	Quinoa porridge	Jalapeño popper bombs	Cheesy Lemon Quinoa Salad	Cocoa peanut butter bombs	Farro Salad with Sweet Pea Pesto	70g
Thursday	High Carb	Cinnamon quinoa with peaches	Vegan Rice Paper Rolls	Rosemary Pasta Shells Soup	Easy Blueberry Muffins	High-Carb Farfalle Pasta with Mushrooms	224g
Friday	High Carb	Apple omelet	Pizza Breadsticks	Asian-Italian Tofu and Capers Pizza	Olive Pizza bombs	Shrimp and Scallop Combo	234g
Saturday	Low Carb	Spinach & Salsa Omelet	Jalapeño popper bombs	Snow Peas & Spaghetti	Thai Tempeh cabbage leaf rolls	Asian Edamame & Tofu Bowl	80g
Sunday	Low Carb	Parmesan and Spinach Frittata	Easy Blueberry Muffins	Spinach Rocket and Avocado Salad	Jalapeño popper bombs	Sunflower Seed Pesto Chicken	70g

WEEK 2

DAY	CARB INTAKE	BREAKFAST	SNACK	LUNCH	SNACK	DINNER	TOTAL CARBS
Monday	High Carb	Golden Flax and Chia	Carrot and Onion muffins	Veggie Stuffed Tomatoes	Crusty Peanut butter bars	Salmon Fettuccini	221g
Tuesday	Moderate Carb	Watercress Cranberry Smoothie	Carrot and Onion muffins	Brussels Carrot & Greens	Sweet Potato Chicken Dumplings	Orange Poached Salmon	135g
Wednesday	Low Carb	Golden Flax and Chia	Freekeh balls	Kale Slaw & Creamy Dressing	Corndog Muffins	Olive Chicken	75g
Thursday	High Carb	Sugar-Free Protein Muesli	Freekeh balls	Rosemary Pasta Shells Soup	Carrot and Onion muffins	Egg Noodles with Croutons	230g
Friday	High Carb	Grape Berry Smoothie	Crusty Peanut butter bars	Bean and Broccoli Chilli	Mini Portobello pizzas	Tortellini Salad with Spinach	230g
Saturday	Low Carb	Golden Flax and Chia	Ham and Cheese Stromboli	Cheesy Lemon Quinoa Salad	Olive Pizza bombs	Turmeric Roasted Cauliflower	73g
Sunday	Low Carb	Bowl of raspberry and almond milk	Jalapeño popper bombs	Caprese Pesto Chicken	Olive Pizza bombs	Garlic and sesame noodles	83g

WEEK 3

DAY	CARB INTAKE	BREAKFAST	SNACK	LUNCH	SNACK	DINNER	TOTAL CARBS
Monday	High Carb	Nut and Seed Granola	Sweet Potato Chicken Dumplings	Mixed fruit salad	Freekeh balls	Egg Noodles with Croutons	217g
Tuesday	Moderate Carb	Berry Cleanser Smoothie	Thai Tempeh cabbage leaf rolls	Spicy Turkey Stir Fry	Mini Portobello pizzas	Tortellini Salad with Spinach	130g
Wednesday	Low Carb	Blueberry Cinnamon Breakfast Bake	Corndog Muffins	Rosemary Pasta Shells Soup	Thai Tempeh cabbage leaf rolls	Roasted Balsamic Chicken	83g
Thursday	High Carb	Sugar-Free Protein Muesli	Sweet Potato Chicken Dumplings	Veggie Stuffed Tomatoes	Pizza Breadsticks	Garlic and sesame noodles	237g
Friday	High Carb	Grape Berry Smoothie	Sweet Potato Chicken Dumplings	Split Peas with Spinach	Carrot and Onion muffins	Tortellini Salad with Spinach	206g
Saturday	Low Carb	Nut and Seed Granola	Ham and Cheese Stromboli	Sea bass with vegetables	Cocoa peanut butter bombs	Fall Pumpkin Soup	80g
Sunday	Low Carb	Pumpkin waffles	Cheddar and Bell pepper pizza	Citrus spinach	Easy Blueberry Muffins	Olive Chicken	75g

WEEK 4

DAY	CARB INTAKE	BREAKFAST	SNACK	LUNCH	SNACK	DINNER	TOTAL CARBS
Monday	High Carb	Cherries dates and apple bowl	Crusty Peanut butter bars	Bean and Broccoli Chilli	Tofu and vegetable skewers	Salmon Fettuccini	235g
Tuesday	Moderate Carb	Parmesan and Spinach Frittata	Vegan Rice Paper Rolls	Lemon prawns	Jalapeño popper bombs	High-Carb Farfalle Pasta with Mushrooms	128g
Wednesday	Low Carb	Blueberry Cinnamon Breakfast Bake	Olive Pizza bombs	Shrimp Mexicana	Ham and Cheese Stromboli	Leftover Turkey Taco Salad	70g
Thursday	High Carb	Berry Cleanser Smoothie	Crusty Peanut butter bars	Mixed fruit salad	Freekeh balls	Fall Pumpkin Soup	208g
Friday	High Carb	Blueberry Cinnamon Breakfast Bake	Tofu and vegetable skewers	Aubergine Chilli	Pizza Breadsticks	Salmon Fettuccini	230g
Saturday	Low Carb	Apple Almond & Coconut Bow	Mini Portobello pizzas	Kale Slaw & Creamy Dressing	Carrot and Onion muffins	Leftover Turkey Taco Salad	77g
Sunday	Low Carb	Quinoa porridge	Sweet Potato Chicken Dumplings	Citrus spinach	Corndog Muffins	Olive Chicken	75g

CHAPTER 6
BREAKFAST

Pumpkin waffles

Makes: 4

NUTRITION: Calories: 369| Fat: 22.5g | Carbohydrates: 31g |Protein: 14.1g

INGREDIENTS:

- 1 teaspoon baking powder
- 1 ½ teaspoons of ground cinnamon
- 3/4 teaspoon of ground ginger
- 1 ½ teaspoons of ground cloves
- 1 ½ teaspoons of ground nutmeg
- 2 tablespoons of olive oil
- 5 organic eggs
- 3/4 cup of almond milk
- 1 ½ cups of pumpkin purée
- 2 bananas that have been peeled and sliced
- a pinch of salt

INSTRUCTIONS:

1. Preheat the waffle maker then grease it.
2. Blend all ingredients until thoroughly combined.
3. Pour into the waffle maker.
4. Cook for approximately 5 minutes.

Spinach & Salsa Omelet

Makes: 1

NUTRITION: Calories: 204 Calories|Carbohydrates: 2.7g|Protein: 17.1g
Fat: 14.1g|Saturated Fat: 5.6g|Sodium: 190mg

INGREDIENTS:

- cup tomatoes and onion salsa
- 1½ cups raw spinach
- 1 tablespoon almond oil
- 2 eggs, beaten
- 1 tablespoon fresh cilantro

INSTRUCTIONS:

1. In a frying skillet, melt the almond oil.
2. Stir in the eggs and spinach in the skillet.
3. Flip the egg once the edge has hardened.
4. Sprinkle the salsa on top.
5. Transfer to a dish and add cilantro as a garnish.

Walnut and almond porridge

Makes: 5

NUTRITION: Calories: 292 | Fat: 7.5g | Carbs: 9.6g | Sodium 75mg | Sugars: 1.2g | Protein: 8g

INGREDIENTS:

- ½ cup pecans
- ¼ cup sunflower seeds
- ¼ cup chia seeds
- Almonds, ½ cup
- ¼ cup coconut flakes(unsweetened)
- 4 cups almond milk(unsweetened)

- ½ teaspoon cinnamon powder
- ¼ teaspoon ginger powder
- 1 teaspoon powdered stevia
- 1 tablespoon almond butter

INSTRUCTIONS:

1. Combine pecans, almonds, and sunflower seeds in a food blender.
2. Boil the nut mixture for about 20 minutes while adding the chia seeds, coconut pieces, almond milk, spices, and stevia powder.
3. Add a spoonful of almond butter before serving.

Spicy Sweet potato Breakfast Bowl

Makes: 4

NUTRITION: Calories 460|Fat 23g|Saturated Fat 9g |Sodium 1000mg |Carbohydrates 24g|Protein 40g

INGREDIENTS:

- Pinch Low-Sodium Salt and pepper
- ½ bell pepper, diced
- chili powder, 1 teaspoon
- 2 sweet potatoes, peeled and diced
- 2 eggs
- ½ onion, diced
- Extra virgin olive oil
- 1 jalapeño, chopped
- fresh spinach, 2-3 cups
- ½ red bell pepper, diced
- 1 avocado, sliced
- Ghee, 1 teaspoon
- 2 strips bacon, cooked and crumbled

INSTRUCTIONS:

1. Heat the oven's temperature to 375 F.
2. On a baking sheet with parchment paper, toss chopped sweet potatoes with olive oil, salt, pepper, and chili powder.
3. Bake for 20 minutes, turning the pan midway.
4. In a pan, sauté the onion, bell peppers, and jalapeno for 6 minutes, or until they are soft.
5. Add and cook the spinach.
6. Melt the ghee in a separate pan.
7. Season with salt and pepper and cook until the eggs are done.
8. Distribute the sweet potatoes among two plates.
9. Add the veggie mixture to the top, then the egg, bacon, and avocado.

Sugar-Free Protein Muesli

Makes: 2

NUTRITION: Energy 399 Calories|Fat 8.20g|Carbohydrates 64.50g |Sugar 11.30g|Protein 20.30g|Sodium 6.8 mg

INGREDIENTS:

- Cinnamon, ½ teaspoon
- coconut flakes, 1 cup
- chopped walnuts, 1 tablespoon
- hemp protein, 1 scoop of
- raw almonds, 1 tablespoon
- dark and sugar-free chocolate chips, 1 tablespoon
- almond milk, 1 cup

INSTRUCTIONS:

1. Layer coconut flakes, walnuts, almonds, and chocolate chips in a bowl.
2. Sprinkle with cinnamon and drizzle almond milk over the muesli.

Parmesan and Spinach Frittata

Makes: 4

NUTRITION: Calories:203| Fat: 17 g | Carbohydrates: 2 |Protein: 13g

INGREDIENTS:

- 2 tablespoons of olive oil
- ½ teaspoons salt
- Parmesan, 2 tablespoons grated
- 2 cups fresh baby spinach
- 8 eggs, beaten
- black pepper, ⅛ teaspoon
- garlic powder, 1 teaspoon

INSTRUCTIONS:

1. Fire up the barbecue.
2. Warm up the olive oil in a pan.
3. After adding the spinach, cook for about 3 minutes while turning occasionally.
4. Mix the eggs, garlic powder, salt, and pepper in a dish.
5. Pour the mixture over the spinach and let it simmer for three minutes.
6. Use a rubber spatula to carefully remove the eggs from the edge of the pan.
7. Top the skillet with Parmesan cheese and place it under the broiler.
8. Bake the sides for 3 minutes, or until golden brown.
9. Cut into serving-size chunks.

Apple, Almond & Coconut Bowl

Makes: 2

NUTRITION: Calories 160 |Fat 12g |Saturated fat 4.5g|Sodium 60mg |Carbohydrates 12g ||Protein 3g

INGREDIENTS:

- 1 Pinch of cinnamon
- sliced almonds, 2 Tablespoons
- ½ apple, cored and roughly diced
- unsweetened coconut, 2 Tablespoons
- 1 pinch of salt

INSTRUCTIONS:

1. Pulse everything in the food processor.
2. Serve with nut milk.

Bowl of raspberry and almond milk

Makes: 3

NUTRITION: Calories: 258 | Fat: 22g | Carbohydrates: 9g | Protein: 11.1g | Sodium 10mg

INGREDIENTS:

- 1 cup frozen raspberries
- ¼ cup collagen peptides
- ¼ cup MCT oil
- 2 tablespoons of chia seeds
- beetroot powder, 1 teaspoon
- vanilla extract, 1 teaspoon
- liquid stevia, 4 drops
- almond milk, 1 ½ cups

INSTRUCTIONS:

1. Blend all ingredients until smooth.
2. Pour into 3 serving bowls and serve with your favorite garnish.

Blueberry Cinnamon Breakfast Bake

Makes: 6

NUTRITION: Calories: 170, 3g Fat, 171mg Sodium, 30g Carbohydrates, 7g Protein

INGREDIENTS:

- 2 teaspoons cinnamon, divided
- 2 eggs, beaten
- Blueberries, 3 cups
- ¼ cup brown sugar, divided
- 8 slices of whole-wheat bread
- Low-fat milk, 1 cup
- Zest of 1 lemon, divided

INSTRUCTIONS:

1. Turn up the Oven's temperature to 350 degrees Fahrenheit.
2. In a dish, combine the cinnamon, eggs, milk, brown sugar, and zest.
3. In a mixing dish, combine the egg mixture, bread, and blueberries.
4. Stir until the majority of the liquid has been absorbed.
5. Fill muffin tins with the mixture.
6. Top the French toast plates with 1 tablespoon brown sugar and 1 teaspoon cinnamon.
7. Cook the French toast for 18 minutes, or until it is done and the top is golden.
8. Cook the remaining 1 cup of blueberries for 10 minutes, or until liquid is released, in a small saucepan with the lemon zest and 1 spoonful of brown sugar.
9. French bread should be topped with crushed blueberries and syrup.

Pork Cracklings With Eggs

Makes: 3

NUTRITION: Calories 421, 43g Fats, 5g Carbohydrates, 27g Protein, Sodium 98 mg

INGREDIENTS:

- 4 slices Bacon, cooked
- 5 Eggs
- 5 ounces pork Rinds
- 1 Tomato
- 1 pinch Salt and Pepper
- ¼ cup Cilantro, chopped
- 1 Avocado
- 2 Jalapeño Peppers, de-seeded
- 1 Onion

INSTRUCTIONS:

1. Fry the pig rinds in the bacon fat.
2. When the pork rinds are crispy, add the vegetables to the skillet.
3. Sauté onions until nearly translucent, then add the chopped cilantro to the pan.
4. Combine all of the ingredients in the skillet with 5 scrambled eggs.
5. Add salt and pepper as desired to season.
6. Cook similar to an omelet.
7. Add diced avocado right before serving.

Nut and Seed Granola

Makes: 2

NUTRITION: Calories 260 | Protein 4.4 grams|Fat 2.9 grams
|Carbohydrates 40.5 grams |Sodium 77 mg

INGREDIENTS:

- ¼ cup sunflower seeds shelled
- 1 cup cashews
- pinch low sodium salt
- ¼ cup pumpkin seeds shelled
- ¾ cup almonds
- ½ cup unsweetened coconut flakes
- a few drops of stevia
- Vanilla, 1 teaspoon

INSTRUCTIONS:

1. Set your oven to 300°F and prepare a baking tray with parchment paper.
2. Combine the pumpkin seeds, cashews, almonds, and coconut shavings.
3. Add vanilla and stevia.
4. Combine the sunflower seeds with the mixture and stir to coat.
5. Apply the mixture evenly to the baking tray, and bake it for 25 minutes.
6. Take off the heat.
7. Season with salt.
8. When it is cool enough to hold, shatter it into pieces.

Golden Flax and Chia

Makes: 1

NUTRITION: Calories 371|Fat 16.5g|Saturated Fat 4.6g|Sodium 875mg
|Carbohydrates 20g|Protein 39g

INGREDIENTS:

- 2 tablespoons almond oil, melted
- ½ cup golden Flax-Meal
- ½ cup Chia seed
- 2 tablespoons dark-ground cinnamon
- 1 tablespoons hemp protein powder
- a few drops of stevia
- 1 teaspoon vanilla extract
- ¾ cup hot water

INSTRUCTIONS:

1. Combine all ingredients.
2. Onto a cookie sheet covered with parchment paper, spread the dough evenly.
3. Bake for 15 minutes at 325 degrees before slicing.
4. Drop the temperature down to 300 and leave for 30 minutes.
5. Remove and separate the pieces.
6. Bake the pieces at 200 degrees F for 1 hour.
7. Enjoy with nut milk!

Italian pizza waffles

Makes: 2

NUTRITION: Calories: 526, 45g Fats, 5g Carbohydrates, 29g Protein

INGREDIENTS:

- Italian Seasoning, 1 teaspoon
- Parmesan Cheese, 4 tablespoons
- Almond Flour, 3 tablespoons
- 4 Eggs
- Bacon Grease, 1 tablespoon
- Psyllium Husk Powder, 1 tablespoon
- Salt and Pepper to Taste
- Tomato Sauce, ½ cup
- Baking Powder, 1 teaspoon
- Cheddar Cheese, 3 ounces
- Pepperoni, 14 slices

INSTRUCTIONS:

1. In a container, combine all ingredients, excluding tomato sauce and cheese, using an immersion blender.
2. Preheat your waffle iron and pour half of the batter into it.
3. Allow cooking for a few minutes.
4. Top each waffle with tomato sauce and cheese.
5. Then, in the oven, broil for 4 minutes.
6. Add pepperoni on top of them if desired.

Nutmeg-Spiced Quinoa porridge

Makes: 4

NUTRITION: Calories: 248 | Fat: 11.4g | Carbs: 30.5g | Protein: 7.4g

INGREDIENTS:

- 1 pinch of ground cloves
- Water, 2 cups
- Cooked red quinoa, 1 cup
- ground ginger, ½ teaspoon
- ½ teaspoon vanilla extract
- ½ cup coconut milk
- ¼ teaspoon fresh lemon zest, finely grated
- 10-12 drops of liquid stevia
- ground cinnamon, 1 teaspoon
- almonds, chopped, 2 tablespoons
- ground nutmeg, ½ teaspoon

INSTRUCTIONS:

1. Combine quinoa and vanilla extract.
2. Add the coconut milk, lemon zest, stevia, and spices to the skillet with the quinoa and stir.
3. Fluff quinoa with a fork.
4. Divide the quinoa mixture evenly among serving bowls.
5. Serve with a garnish of chopped almonds.

CHAPTER 7
LUNCH

Black Pepper Salmon with yogurt

Makes: 4

NUTRITION: Calories: 313| Fat: 18.3g | Carbs: 1.4g | Protein: 34g

INGREDIENTS:

- ¼ teaspoon cayenne powder
- ½ teaspoon coriander powder
- ½ teaspoon ginger powder
- ½ teaspoon turmeric powder
- Greek yogurt, ¼ cup

- Pinch Salt
- Pinch ground black pepper

SALMON
- 4 skinless salmon fillets

INSTRUCTIONS:

1. Warm up the grill or broiler.
2. Arrange the salmon fillets on the broiler plate in a single layer.
3. Combine all the marinade ingredients and evenly distribute the yogurt mixture over each fillet.
4. Broil for about 15 minutes.

Cheesy Lemon Quinoa Salad

Makes: 4

NUTRITION: 250 Calories|9g Fat |4g Saturated|262mg Sodium | 33g Carbohydrates|9g Protein

INGREDIENTS:

- Pinch teaspoon salt
- olive oil, 2 tablespoons
- 1 small yellow bell pepper, diced
- 1 teaspoon black pepper
- 1 cucumber diced
- Juice of ½ lemon

- 1 tablespoon dill, chopped
- 1 cup reduced-fat feta cheese, crumbled
- 2 cloves garlic, pressed
- 1 cup quinoa, cooked
- 1 cup cherry tomatoes, quartered

INSTRUCTIONS:

1. Whisk olive oil, garlic, lemon juice, salt, and pepper.
2. Toss everything with the dressing.

Prawns with asparagus

Makes: 4

NUTRITION: Calories: 241| Fat: 9.2g | Carbohydrates: 9.8g | Protein: 30.7g

INGREDIENTS:

- 1 bunch of asparagus, peeled and sliced or diced
- 1-pound shrimp, peeled and deveined
- cup chicken broth
- 4 garlic cloves, crushed
- ground ginger, ½ teaspoon
- lemon juice, 2 tablespoons
- almond oil, 2 tablespoons

INSTRUCTIONS:

1. The almond oil should be melted in a pan over medium heat.
2. Add all the ingredients (aside from the broth) and simmer for two minutes.
3. Cook for about 5 minutes while stirring.
4. Include the broth and simmer for two to four minutes.

Spinach, Rocket, and Avocado Salad

Makes: 3-4

NUTRITION: 94 Calories|16.4g carbohydrate |15.5g protein

INGREDIENTS:

- baby spinach, 8 cups
- 1 onion
- Avocado or olive oil
- ½ chopped avocado
- Juice of ½ lemon
- 1 handful rocket
- 1 pinch of Himalayan salt & black pepper

INSTRUCTIONS:

1. Thoroughly wash all of the vegetables before placing them in a large salad bowl.
2. Finely cut the avocado, thinly slice the red onion, and combine it with the vegetables.
3. After adding the lemon juice to the lettuce, drizzle some oil over it.
4. Season with salt and pepper to flavor.

Caprese Pesto Chicken

Makes: 4

NUTRITION: 248 Calories|10g Fat (2g Saturated) |314mg Sodium |19g Carbohydrates |25g Protein

INGREDIENTS:

- 2 medium boneless, skinless chicken breasts, sliced
- 1 cup packed fresh basil leaves
- 2 tablespoons raw, hulled sunflower seeds
- 2 tablespoons grated parmesan cheese
- 1 clove garlic, chopped
- teaspoon salt
- teaspoon black pepper
- ¼ cup olive oil
- 2 tomatoes, sliced
- ¼ cup shredded part-skim mozzarella cheese, divided

INSTRUCTIONS:

1. Heat the oven's temperature to 425 F.
2. Combine basil, sunflower seeds, parmesan cheese, garlic, salt, and pepper in a food processor.
3. Pulse a few times to combine. While the machine is operating, slowly drizzle in the oil until the sauce is smooth.
4. Top each piece of chicken with 2 teaspoons of pesto, 2 tomato slices, and 1 tablespoon of mozzarella.
5. Bake for 14 minutes, or until fully cooked.

Rosemary Pasta Shells Soup

Makes: 4

NUTRITION: Calories 218.4, Fat 3.3 g, Carbohydrates 37.9 g, Protein 12 g

INGREDIENTS:

- 2 teaspoons olive oil
- Pinch red pepper flakes
- ½ cup whole wheat pasta shells
- 1 shallot, finely diced
- 1 garlic clove, pressed

- 14.5-ounce can of white beans
- Baby Spinach, 3 Cups
- black pepper, 1/8 teaspoon
- fat-free chicken broth, 4 cups
- Dried rosemary, 1 teaspoon
- can of diced tomatoes, 14.5-ounces

INSTRUCTIONS:

1. Turn up the Oven's temperature to 350°F.
2. Warm the oil, then cook the onion and garlic for 4 minutes.
3. Include the beans, tomatoes, rosemary, black and red pepper, as desired, and stock.
4. Bring to a boil.
5. Add the noodles.
6. Finally, stir in the spinach and simmer for 5 minutes.

Mixed fruit salad

Makes: 10

NUTRITION: Calories: 161| Fat: 0.6g | Carbohydrates: 41.6g | Protein: 1.7g | Sodium: 8mg

INGREDIENTS:

- 5 cups pineapple, peeled, cored, and chopped
- 2 oranges, peeled and sliced
- 2 Fuji apples, cored and chopped
- 2 mangoes, peeled, pitted, and chopped
- 2 red Bartlett pears, cored and chopped

DRESSING
- 2 tablespoons of raw honey
- 2 teaspoons fresh ginger, finely grated
- ¼ cup fresh lemon juice

INSTRUCTIONS:

1. Put all the vegetables and fruit in a bowl.
2. In a mixing bowl, combine the dressing ingredients and whisk them well.
3. Toss the fruit with the dressing until it is well coated.

Snow Peas & Spaghetti

Makes: 6

NUTRITION: Calories 337.1|Fat 9.5g|Sodium 477.5mg
|Carbohydrates 38.9g|Protein 22.7g

INGREDIENTS:

- 2 tablespoons sesame oil, divided
- 3/8 teaspoon ground ginger, pressed
- ½ teaspoon crushed red pepper flakes
- 1 tablespoon cornstarch
- 1 tablespoon canola oil
- 1 tablespoon sugar
- 2 cups fresh snow peas

- 4 tablespoons reduced-sodium soy sauce,
- 2 cups carrots, shredded
- 1 lb. boneless skinless chicken breast
- 8 ounces spaghetti, cooked
- 2 tablespoons white vinegar
- 3 green onions, chopped

INSTRUCTIONS:

1. Combine the chicken, corn starch, sesame oil, and half the soy sauce in a zip-top container. Shake the bag to coat it.
2. Leave it alone for 20 minutes so the tastes can meld.
3. In a pan over medium-high heat, warm the canola oil. Cook the chicken for 8 minutes before adding the carrots, peas, green onions, ginger, and pepper flakes.
4. Combine the vinegar, sugar, sesame oil, and leftover soy sauce.
5. Add the pasta, and vinegar mixture to the pan and cook together for two minutes before serving.

Brussels, Carrot & Greens

Makes: 2

NUTRITION: Calories 704| Carbs 88g| Fat 37g| Protein 20g
|Carbs 57g| Sodium 2174mg

INGREDIENTS:

- 2 cloves of garlic
- Zest of 1 lemon
- Olive oil
- 1 broccoli

- 2 carrots, sliced thin
- 6 brussels sprouts
- caraway seeds, 1 teaspoon
- ½ lemon

INSTRUCTIONS:

1. Steam all the vegetables for 8 minutes on low heat.
2. Sauté garlic with caraway seeds, lemon peel, lemon juice, and olive oil.
3. Add the carrot and Brussels sprouts.

Lemon prawns

Makes: 6

NUTRITION: Calories: 268| Fat: 20.6g | Carbohydrates: 4.2g | Protein: 17.2g | Sodium: 94.4mg

INGREDIENTS:

- 1 onion, diced
- 1 teaspoon ground turmeric
- 1 tablespoon almond oil
- 3 garlic cloves, crushed
- 1 tablespoon fresh lemon zest, finely grated
- 1 fresh red pepper, seeded and chopped
- ½ cup olive oil
- lemon juice, ½ cup
- 1 tablespoon fresh ginger, chopped
- 20-24 raw shrimp, peeled and deveined

INSTRUCTIONS:

1. Combine all the ingredients—aside from the shrimp and almond oil—in a dish.
2. Add the shrimp and toss it with the marinade.
3. Marinate in the refrigerator overnight with a cover.
4. In a nonstick pan over high heat, melt the almond oil, then sauté the shrimp for three minutes.
5. Add any remaining marinade, and while stirring periodically, bring to a boil.
6. Cook for 1-2 minutes.

Veggie-Stuffed Tomatoes

Makes: 4

NUTRITION: Calories. 109; Fat. 2.65 g; Carbs. 19.55 g; Protein. 2.41 g

INGREDIENTS:

- 1 tablespoon cold-pressed oil
- 2 tomatoes
- 1 Pinch of sea salt and pepper
- Half a small aubergine
- 1 onion
- ⅓ of a courgette
- 1-2 cloves of garlic
- 1 bunch of fresh spinach leaves

INSTRUCTIONS:

1. Preheat the oven to 160 degrees Celsius (325 degrees Fahrenheit).
2. Toss vegetables with spinach, salt, pepper, and oil.
3. After that, place the tomatoes on top and scoop out the center. Combine the middle piece with the rest of the mixture and stir well.
4. Now you must carefully place everything back into the tomatoes.
5. Put the tomatoes in a pan with water and cover them with a lid.
6. Bake for 18 minutes.

Shrimp Mexicana

Makes: 4

NUTRITION: Calories 12|Fat 0.3g grams|Saturated Fat 0.1g grams |Carbohydrates 0.5g grams|Protein 1g

INGREDIENTS:

FOR THE TORTILLAS:
- 6 egg whites
- the low sodium salt, ½ teaspoon
- coconut flour, ¼ cup
- almond milk, ¼ cup
- Cumin, ½ teaspoon
- chili powder, ¼ teaspoon

FOR THE SHRIMP:
- 1 lime, cut into wedges
- extra-virgin olive oil, 1 tablespoon
- Shredded lettuce, for serving
- chili powder, 1 teaspoon
- Salt, 1 teaspoon
- 1 lb. medium shrimp, peeled and deveined
- 1 avocado, pitted and diced
- Fresh cilantro, for serving

INSTRUCTIONS:

1. Heat a skillet over medium heat, add the salt, chili pepper, and olive oil, and toss the shrimp in the mixture to coat. Place away.
2. Whisk the ingredients for the tortillas to make the batter.
3. Spray the skillet with almond oil spray before adding a thin coating of batter.
4. Cook for two minutes before turning over and cooking for an additional two minutes, or until faintly browned.
5. Serve shrimp, lettuce, avocado, and cilantro, on a tortilla.

Kale Slaw & Creamy Dressing

Makes: 2

NUTRITION: 97 Calories| 5.7g Carbs|6.8g fat|1.7g protein

INGREDIENTS:

- ⅓ cup sesame seeds
- 1 bell pepper
- ⅓ cup sunflower seeds
- 1 red onion

- 1 bunch of kale
- 4 cups of red cabbage, shredded
- 1 piece of root ginger
- Fresh coriander
- 1 Serving of cashew dressing

INSTRUCTIONS:

1. Toss all the ingredients together.

Bean and Broccoli Chilli

Makes: 2

NUTRITION: Calories: 243; Protein: 13.1 g; Carbohydrate: 49 g; Sugar: 5.6 g; Fat: 1.3 g

INGREDIENTS:

- 1 bunch of spinach
- Himalayan Salt and Freshly cracked black pepper
- tomato purée, 2 tablespoons
- olive oil, 1 tablespoon
- 1 onion, chopped
- 1 garlic clove, crushed
- 1 red chili, thinly sliced
- ground cumin, ½ teaspoons
- ground coriander, ½ teaspoon
- 1 can of red kidney beans, drained
- 1 head of broccoli, chopped small
- 1 can of chopped tomatoes
- Wedges of lime, to serve
- ½ yeast-free veg stock cube
- 1 Dash Liquid Aminos

INSTRUCTIONS:

1. Heat stock and steam the onion and garlic.
2. Add the stock cube, tomatoes, tomato purée, chili, cumin, coriander, Aminos sauce, salt, and pepper.
3. Simmer for about 20 minutes.
4. Combine the kidney beans and fresh coriander in a mixing bowl and cook for another 9 minutes.
5. Top with raw broccoli and spinach, as well as avocado or olive oil.

Citrus spinach

Makes: 4

NUTRITION: Calories: 80| Fat: 7 g | Carbohydrates: 4g |Protein: 1g

INGREDIENTS:

- 2 tablespoons olive oil (extra-virgin)
- Juice of ½ orange
- The zest of ½ an orange
- baby spinach, 4 cups
- ⅛ teaspoon black pepper, freshly ground
- 2 garlic cloves, crushed
- ½ teaspoons sea salt

INSTRUCTIONS:

1. In a pan, warm the olive oil.
2. Include greens and cook for three minutes.
3. Add garlic right away. Stirring continuously, cook for 30 seconds.
4. Include the orange juice, peel, salt, and pepper.
5. Cook, stirring continuously, for 2 minutes or until juices have disappeared.

Aubergine Chilli

Makes: 4

NUTRITION: Calories 394 | Fat 14.1g| Saturates 1.3g| Carbs 39.8g | Sugars 19.4g | Protein 15.2g | Salt 0.1g

INGREDIENTS:

- 1 red onion, finely chopped
- 1 aubergine cut into cubes
- 2 garlic cloves, crushed
- 2 cups black beans, cooked
- 5 small red chilies, chopped
- cinnamon powder, 1 teaspoon
- coriander powder, ½ teaspoons
- cumin powder, 1 teaspoon
- Coconut oil or olive oil
- 1 can of tomatoes
- Sea salt
- Freshly cracked black pepper
- 2 serves of brown rice, quinoa, or couscous

INSTRUCTIONS:

1. Fry the aubergines for 4 minutes in melted coconut oil. Place away.
2. Sauté the shallots, garlic, and chiles for a total of 4 minutes.
3. Cook the aubergine for 5 minutes after adding the tomatoes, coriander, and spices.
4. After putting in the black beans, simmer for 9 minutes.

Split Peas with Spinach

Makes: 4

NUTRITION: Calories: 215 | Fat: 7 g | Saturated Fat: 1.0 g | Sodium: 128 Mg | Carbohydrate: 36 g | Protein: 7 g

INGREDIENTS:

- 2 plum tomatoes, chopped
- 4 cups water
- 2 garlic cloves, pressed
- 1 teaspoon Low-Sodium Salt
- ground cumin1 teaspoon
- ginger, finely chopped, 1 tablespoon
- ground coriander, ½ teaspoon
- Turmeric. ½ teaspoon
- 2 cups fresh baby spinach
- 1cup yellow split peas, rinsed and drained
- 1 serrano chile, seeded and pressed
- chopped fresh cilantro, 1/4 cup
- canola oil, 1 tablespoon
- 2 teaspoons fresh lemon juice

INSTRUCTIONS:

1. Boil the peas for 40 minutes or until they are tender.
2. Add the tomatoes and greens and stir. Set aside.
3. In a pan with hot oil, sauté the garlic, ginger, and chile for one minute.
4. Season with lemon juice, cumin, coriander, and turmeric.
5. Add the combination to the dal and stir. Then, serve.

Spicy Turkey Stir Fry

Makes: 3

NUTRITION: 233 calories| 6g fat (1g saturated fat) |866mg sodium | 13g carbohydrate | 33g protein

INGREDIENTS:

- freshly ground pepper, 2 teaspoons
- 1 teaspoon garam masala
- 2 bell peppers, thinly sliced
- coconut oil, 2 tablespoons
- Pinch low sodium salt
- 2 lbs. boneless skinless turkey breasts, sliced
- 1 teaspoon cumin seeds

FOR THE MARINADE:
- 1 clove of garlic, pressed
- 1 teaspoon low sodium salt
- ½ cup coconut cream
- ¼ teaspoon turmeric
- 1 teaspoon ginger, pressed

INSTRUCTIONS:

1. Combine the marinade ingredients with the chicken and set aside for 1 hour.
2. Melt the coconut oil in a wok or large sauté pan over medium-high heat.
3. Next, add the cumin seeds and simmer for 3 minutes.
4. After adding the marinated chicken, cook for 5 minutes and then stir in the peppers, garam masala, and pepper.
5. Add a pinch of low-sodium salt to taste.
6. Cook for 5 minutes, stirring regularly.

Bell pasta with kidney beans

Makes: 8

NUTRITION: Calories 174 kcal |Fat 3.1 g | Carbohydrates 29g | Protein 8g | Sodium 190.3mg

INGREDIENTS:

- 3 Cups chicken broth
- 2 cloves garlic, pressed
- 1 Pinch of ground black pepper to taste
- 1 cup seashell pasta
- 1 onion, chopped
- chopped fresh thyme, 2 teaspoons
- 1 cup whole tomatoes, chopped
- chopped spinach, ½ cup
- 1 red bell pepper, chopped
- 2 cups kidney beans, cooked
- olive oil1 tablespoon

INSTRUCTIONS:

1. Get a saucepan ready.
2. Heat the oil, add the onion, bell pepper, and garlic, and sauté for 3 minutes.
3. Add the beans, stock, and tomatoes; simmer for 20 minutes.
4. Add the linguine, spinach, and thyme, and cook for an additional 5 minutes.
5. Add salt and pepper for seasoning.

Sea bass with vegetables

Makes: 2

NUTRITION: Calories: 280| Fat: 17.6g | Carbs: 8.8g | Sodium: 76.5mg | Sugars: 3.8g | Protein: 23.9g

INGREDIENTS:

- 1 sea bass fillet, diced
- 1 tablespoon coconut vinegar
- ¼ teaspoon garlic paste
- 1 teaspoon red pepper powder
- fish sauce, 1 teaspoon
- 1 tablespoon olive oil, extra-virgin
- ½ cup fresh button mushrooms, sliced
- 1 small onion, quartered
- ¼ cup yellow bell peppers, seeded and diced
- ¼ teaspoon ginger paste
- ¼ cup red bell pepper, seeded and diced
- Pinch of salt
- 2-3 spring onions, chopped

INSTRUCTIONS:

1. Mix the fish with the salt, chili pepper, ginger, and garlic in a bowl and set aside for 20 minutes.
2. In a skillet that has been heated with 1 teaspoon of oil, sear the salmon for 4 minutes on each side. Place away.
3. Heat the leftover oil, then sauté the mushrooms and shallots for about 6 minutes.
4. Add the fish sauce and spring onions, then simmer for about 3 minutes.

Vegetable Pasta

Makes: 4

NUTRITION: Calories 160| Fat 3g | Carbohydrate 30g| Protein 8g

INGREDIENTS:

- Himalayan salt and black pepper
- 1 courgette
- 5 garlic gloves
- Chilies, diced
- ½ pack of vegetable or spelt pasta, cooked
- 4 tomatoes
- A handful of basil leaves
- 1 medium broccoli
- 1 tablespoon of olive oil

INSTRUCTIONS:

1. Heat the oil on low, gentle heat, and sauté the garlic, basil, and chili for two minutes.
2. Add the remaining vegetables, which have been sliced to make them tiny and easy to cook.
3. Cook everything for another two minutes.

Squash and Lentil Soup

Makes: 4-6

NUTRITION: Calories: 167|Fat: 5g|Saturated: 1g|Carbohydrate: 23g |Protein: 6g

INGREDIENTS:

- 1 bay leaf
- 8 cups of vegetable broth
- 1 large onion, diced
- 1 cup brown lentils
- 2 teaspoons pressed garlic
- 1 peeled and diced butternut squash
- ground nutmeg, ½ teaspoon
- 1 cup spinach, chopped
- ½ teaspoon of salt

INSTRUCTIONS:

1. Add all ingredients, excluding the spinach, to your slow cooker and mix well.
2. Simmer for 8 hours.
3. Remove the bay leaf.
4. Add chopped spinach and stir until softened.

Rigatoni Pasta Casserole

Makes: 6

NUTRITION: Calories 795.6, Fat 37.6 g, Sodium 1842.2 mg, Carbohydrates 73.2, Protein 41.2 g

INGREDIENTS:

- 14-ounce can of cannellini beans, drained and rinsed
- 1 lb. ground sausage
- 16-ounce rigatoni pasta, cooked
- 1/4 cup Romano cheese, grated
- 28-ounce can of Italian-style tomato sauce
- Parsley, to garnish
- 1/2 teaspoon garlic, pressed
- 3 cups shredded mozzarella cheese
- Italian seasoning, 1 teaspoon

INSTRUCTIONS:

1. Turn up the oven's temperature to 350°F.
2. Grease a baking dish with butter or oil.
3. After browning the meats and garlic for six minutes, add the tomato sauce, beans, and Italian seasoning. Simmer for five more minutes.
4. Pour half of the sausage pasta combination and half of the mozzarella cheese into the prepared casserole. Repeat the procedure to create other layers.
5. Cover the casserole with foil and sprinkle Romano cheese on top.
6. Bake for 26 minutes.

Coconut Ground Beef

Makes: 5

NUTRITION: Calories: 352| Fat: 22.8g | Carbs: 8.1g | Protein: 29.4g

INGREDIENTS:

- 2 bay leaves
- 2 whole cloves
- 1 teaspoon of cumin
- 2 whole cardamoms
- 1-pound lean ground beef
- 2 onions, chopped
- Pinch of salt
- garlic paste, ½ Tablespoons
- Water, ¼ cup

- fresh ginger paste, ½ Tablespoon
- red chili powder, 1½ teaspoons
- coconut milk, 1 cup
- coconut oil, 2 tablespoons
- cinnamon stick, 1 piece
- ground cumin, 1 teaspoon
- ground turmeric, ⊠ teaspoon
- black pepper, freshly ground
- ground fennel seeds, 1½ teaspoons
- fresh cilantro, chopped, ¼ cup

INSTRUCTIONS:

1. In a pan over high heat, add the oil and cook the bay leaves, cumin, cardamom, cloves, and cinnamon stick for 20 to 30 seconds.
2. Sauté the onion for 3 to 4 minutes while adding 2 teaspoons of salt.
3. Add the ginger puree and the garlic, and cook for another two minutes.
4. Add meat and cook the meat for approximately 4-5 minutes, breaking it up with a spatula as it cooks.
5. Cook for about 5 minutes with the lid off.
6. Add the seasonings and stir continuously for about 2 to 2 12 minutes.
7. Add the coconut milk and water, stir, and then simmer for 7-8 minutes.
8. Add salt and turn off the fire.
9. Garnish with cilantro before serving fresh.

CHAPTER 8
DINNER

Sunflower Seed Pesto Chicken

Makes: 4

NUTRITION: 246 Calories|10g Fat |2g Saturated|314mg Sodium | 19g Carbohydrates|25g Protein

INGREDIENTS:

CHICKEN
• 2 boneless, skinless chicken breasts, sliced lengthwise

PESTO
• 2 tablespoons parmesan cheese, grated
• 1 clove of garlic, chopped
• 2 tablespoons raw, hulled sunflower seeds

• olive oil, ¼ cup
• black pepper, ⅛ teaspoon
• Salt, ⅛ teaspoon
• 1 cup basil leaves

GARNISHES
• ¼ cup part-skim mozzarella cheese, shredded and divided
• 2 tomatoes, sliced

INSTRUCTIONS:

1. Arrange the chicken on an oiled baking sheet with a rim.
2. In a food processor, whirl the components for the pesto.
3. Spread mozzarella, tomato slices, and pesto on top of the poultry.
4. Bake for 15 minutes and serve hot.

Farro Salad with Sweet Pea Pesto

Makes: 8

NUTRITION: 201 Calories|10g Fat |2g Saturated| 86mg Sodium | 23g Carbohydrates|7g Protein

INGREDIENTS:

• 2 cups cherry or grape tomatoes
• ¼ cup parmesan cheese
• Zest of 1 lemon
• 2 cups peas
• ½ cup low-sodium canned white beans
• 2 cloves garlic

• Hulled sunflower seeds, 2 tablespoons
• black pepper, 1 teaspoon
• olive oil, ¼ cup
• 1 cup farro, cooked and cooled
• 1 bell pepper, diced

INSTRUCTIONS:

1. Pulse peas, parmesan, garlic, sunflower seeds, and pepper until the peas are finely pressed; slowly drip in the olive oil.
2. Combine everything in a mixing dish.

Leftover Turkey Taco Salad

Makes: 2

NUTRITION: Calories 292.5|Fat 6.0 g|Saturated Fat 1.8 g |Sodium 1,198.7 mg|Carbohydrate 29.2 g|Protein 31.1 g

INGREDIENTS:

- 1 tablespoon coconut or olive oil
- ½ lb. leftover turkey, cooked and chopped
- 1 ½ tablespoons taco seasoning
- ¼ cup water
- 1 tablespoon of rice vinegar
- Shredded lettuce

TACO SEASONING:
- red pepper flakes, 1 teaspoon
- garlic powder, 1 teaspoon
- paprika, 2 teaspoons
- onion powder, 1 teaspoon

- Oregano, 1 teaspoon
- chili powder, 3 tablespoons
- Cumin, 2 teaspoons
- low-sodium salt, 4 teaspoons

TOPPINGS
- Red Onion
- Sliced Olives
- Tomatoes
- Avocado
- Bell Peppers
- Crushed Sweet Potato Chips

INSTRUCTIONS:

1. In a skillet, heat oil and add the chicken; cook until the liquid has evaporated, stirring in the water and taco seasoning.
2. Prepare all of your toppings by shredding, chopping, and dicing them.
3. Combine lettuce, toppings, chicken, remaining oil and vinegar dressing, and smashed chips in a salad bowl.

High-Carb Farfalle Pasta with Mushrooms

Makes: 4

NUTRITION: Calories 720 kcal, Carbohydrates 92.8 g, Fat 32.9 g, Protein 18.1 g, Sodium 490 mg

INGREDIENTS:

- 8-ounce pack of mushrooms, sliced
- Butter, ¼ cup
- 1 lb. farfalle pasta, cooked
- Pinch salt and pepper to taste
- 2 zucchinis, quartered and sliced
- ⅓ cup olive oil

- 1 tablespoon paprika
- 1 tablespoon dried oregano
- 1 onion, chopped
- 1 clove of garlic, chopped
- 1 tomato, chopped

INSTRUCTIONS:

1. Sauté tomato, onion, mushrooms, and garlic for 17 minutes in olive oil.
2. Season with oregano, paprika, salt, and pepper.
3. Toss the vegetables and noodles and serve.

Shrimp and Scallop Combo

Makes: 4-6

NUTRITION: Calories 668| Fat 18g (Saturated 8g) | Sodium 602mg| Carbohydrate 75g| Protein 56g.

INGREDIENTS:

- chopped scallions, ½ cup
- 1 cup broccoli florets, steamed in the microwave
- ½ cup soy milk
- clarified butter, divided, 4 tablespoons
- 1 clove of garlic, pressed or pressed
- ½ cup vegetable broth
- 1-pound jumbo raw shrimp peeled and deveined

- 1-pound bay scallops
- chopped basil, 3 tablespoons
- chopped parsley, 2 tablespoons
- Marjoram, 1 teaspoon
- 2 tablespoons spelt flour
- ½ cup green bell peppers, seeded and diced
- 2 cups diced tomatoes
- 12 ounces cooked spelt or vegetable pasta

INSTRUCTIONS:

1. Sauté the bell peppers, onions, and garlic in 2 teaspoons of melted butter for 5 minutes.
2. Add the veggie broth and heat it through until it has completely evaporated.
3. Cook and drain the pasta as directed on the package, then put it aside.
4. In a saucepan, slowly bring the soy milk to a boil.
5. Stir in the spelt flour as the mixture begins to stiffen.
6. In a skillet set over medium heat, melt the leftover butter.
7. Add the basil, parsley, marjoram, shrimp, and scallops in a mixing dish.
8. Stirring gently, cook the shellfish for 3 minutes with the lid off.
9. Toss all of the seasonings with the cooked pasta before serving.

Lettuce and Spinach Herb Salad

Makes: 3-4

NUTRITION: 84 Calories| Protein 4.5g| Carbohydrates 4g| Fat 6g | Saturated Fat 1.2g | Sodium 113mg

INGREDIENTS:

- Lambs leaf lettuce, torn
- 2 spring onions, sliced
- Fresh coriander
- Juice of a ½ lemon

- 1 bunch of baby spinach leaves
- Fresh parsley
- Romaine lettuce, torn
- Fennel
- Olive oil

INSTRUCTIONS:

1. In a mixing dish, combine all the ingredients.

Orange Poached Salmon

Makes: 3

NUTRITION: Calories 160| Fat 3g | Carbohydrate 30g| Protein 8g

INGREDIENTS:

- 1 teaspoon ginger, pressed
- ½ cup fresh orange juice
- 3 tablespoons coconut aminos
- 4 garlic cloves, crushed
- 3 salmon fillets

INSTRUCTIONS:

1. Heat the oil on low, gentle heat, and sauté the garlic, basil, and chili for two minutes.
2. Add the remaining vegetables, which have been sliced to make them tiny and easy to cook.
3. Cook everything for another two minutes.

Mango, Jalapeño & bean salad

Makes: 6

NUTRITION: Calories: 215, Fat: 7 g (Saturated Fat: 1.0 g), Sodium: 128 Mg, Carbohydrate: 36 g, Protein: 7 g

INGREDIENTS:

- 1 bell pepper, seeded, diced
- 1 cup avocado, cubed
- 2 tablespoons lime juice
- 1 teaspoon Low-Sodium Salt
- 2 green onions, sliced
- 15-ounce can, of low-sodium whole-kernel corn
- olive oil, 1 tablespoon

- 1 teaspoon chili powder
- 1 jalapeño pepper, diced
- 15-ounce can of black beans, drained
- 2 mangos, cut into ½-inch cubes
- 2 tablespoons fresh cilantro, chopped
- 1 teaspoon black pepper
- Shredded lettuce

INSTRUCTIONS:

1. Distribute greens among the six plates.
2. Combine the corn, mango, avocado, onions, jalapenos, and black beans.
3. In a container with a tight-fitting lid, combine the lime juice, olive oil, cilantro, chili powder, black pepper, and salt by violently shaking the ingredients.
4. Pour dressing over lettuce and mixed greens and toss lightly to combine.
5. Add the mango-avocado combination on top.

Salmon Fettuccini

Makes: 6

NUTRITION: Calories 524| Fat 12g (Saturated 3g) | Sodium 233mg | Carbohydrate 76g| Protein 35g

INGREDIENTS:

- 12 ounces fresh salmon fillets
- spelt fettuccini, cooked, 12 ounces
- 20 spinach leaves
- Sea salt and pepper to taste

- clarified butter, 1 tablespoon
- Fresh basil
- Lemon juice, 3 tablespoons
- 2 cloves garlic, pressed

INSTRUCTIONS:

1. Fire up the barbecue.
2. Gently season the salmon with salt and pepper before grilling it for 6 minutes on each side.
3. Warm up the butter, lemon juice, and garlic to make the sauce.
4. Combine linguine, spinach, garlic-butter sauce, and fresh basil in a serving bowl.

Stewed Cashew Vegetables

Makes: 3

NUTRITION: Calories: 425| Fat: 32g | Carbohydrates: 27.6g | Protein: 13.4g

INGREDIENTS:

- broccoli florets. 1½ cup
- cauliflower florets. 1½ cup
- olive oil. 2 tablespoons
- 1 onion. sliced
- lemon juice, freshly squeezed, 1 tablespoon
- fresh lemon zest, grated, 1 teaspoon
- fresh ginger, grated, ¼ teaspoon
- 2 garlic cloves, pressed
- Pinch salt and black pepper
- vegetable broth, 2 cups
- cayenne pepper, 1 teaspoon
- Cashews, 1 pound
- cumin powder, 1 teaspoon

INSTRUCTIONS:

1. In about three minutes, sauté the onion in oil.
2. Include seasonings, ginger, and garlic.
3. Boil for 1 cup while adding stock.
4. Include the veggies and re-boil.
5. Cook with the cover on for 15 to 20 minutes, stirring occasionally.
6. After adding the lemon juice, turn off the heat.
7. Garnish the hot dish with lemon zest and cashew seeds.

Garlic and sesame noodles

Makes: 4

NUTRITION: Calories 524| Fat 12g (Saturated 3g) | Sodium 233mg | Carbohydrate 76g| Protein 35g

INGREDIENTS:

- 1-pound brown rice spaghetti, cooked
- toasted sesame oil, 1½ tablespoons
- sliced green onions, 1 cup
- red pepper flakes, ½ teaspoon
- 7 garlic cloves, crushed
- soy sauce, ¼ cup
- hazelnut sugar, ¼ cup
- rice vinegar, 2 tablespoons
- Sesame seeds for garnish

INSTRUCTIONS:

1. Over low to medium heat, heat a skillet.
2. Pour in the sesame oil and once heated, stir in ¾ cup of green onions, garlic, and red pepper flakes.
3. Cook until garlic is lightly browned and fragrant, stirring frequently to avoid burning.
4. Add soy sauce, coconut sugar, and rice vinegar and stir to combine. Add the prepared, drained pasta and toss to coat with the sauce.
5. Cook for 2 minutes.
6. Serve garnished with the leftover sesame seeds and green onions.

Tortellini Salad with Spinach

Makes: 2

NUTRITION: Calories 716 kcal, Fat 39g, Carbohydrates 66g,
Protein 29 g, Sodium 1027 mg

INGREDIENTS:

- 9-ounce package of spinach and cheese
- 1 jar tortellini, cooked
- 4-ounce jar pesto
- halved, seeded, and sliced cucumber, ¼ cup
- ¼ cup red onion, diced
- halved cherry tomatoes, ¼ cup
- ½ Cup chopped mache

INSTRUCTIONS:

1. Place the cucumbers, tomatoes, onions, tortellini, and mache on top of the pesto in the jar.
2. Serve or refrigerate until ready to eat.

Cod in tomato sauce

Makes: 5

NUTRITION: Calories:303| Fat: 7.9g | Carbohydrates: 12.2g
| Protein: 45.2g | Sodium: 329.6mg

INGREDIENTS:

- olive oil, 2 tablespoons
- tomato paste, 3 tablespoons
- dried dill weed, 1 teaspoon
- ground cumin, 1½ teaspoons
- 2 jalapeño peppers, chopped
- turmeric powder, 1 teaspoon
- Sumac, 2 teaspoons
- 1 sweet onion, diced
- 8 garlic cloves, crushed
- 2 tablespoons lime juice
- ground coriander, 2 teaspoons
- 5 medium tomatoes, chopped
- ½ cup of water
- 5 cod fillets
- 1 Pinch Low-Sodium Salt and black pepper

INSTRUCTIONS:

1. To make the spice mixture, combine the dill and the other ingredients in a dish.
2. In a pan that has been heated, add the onion and cook for about 2 minutes.
3. Sauté the garlic and jalapeno for about 2 minutes.
4. Add the water, half the spice mixture, salt, and pepper, along with the tomatoes, tomato puree, lime juice, and remaining spices. Bring to a boil.
5. Cook, covered, over medium-low heat for approximately 10 minutes, turning occasionally.
6. Evenly season the cod fillets with salt, pepper, and the leftover spice mixture.
7. Add the fish fillets to the tomato mixture in the wok and gently press them down.
8. Turn the heat to medium-high and prepare the food for around two minutes.
9. Covered, simmer for approximately 15 minutes.

Ginger Tilapia

Makes: 5

NUTRITION: Calories: 266| Fat: 8.8g | Carbohydrates: 19.9g | Protein: 29.1g | Sodium: 895.8mg

INGREDIENTS:

- 2 tablespoons coconut aminos
- 5 tilapia fillets
- 2 tablespoons fresh ginger, chopped
- 2 tablespoons unsweetened coconut, grated
- 3 garlic cloves, crushed
- 8 spring onions, chopped
- 2 tablespoons almond oil

INSTRUCTIONS:

1. Melt the almond oil in a pan over high heat, then cook the tilapia fillets for about two minutes on each side.
2. Cook for one minute after adding the coconut, ginger, and garlic.
3. Stir in the coconut aminos and continue to simmer for another minute.
4. Add the spring onion and continue cooking for an additional two minutes.

Roasted Balsamic Chicken

Makes: 4

NUTRITION: 182 Calories | 7 g Fat (2 g Saturated Fat) | 4g Carbohydrates | 25g Protein | 131mg Sodium

INGREDIENTS:

- 4 chicken thighs
- lemon juice, 1 tablespoon
- olive oil, 2 tablespoons
- 2 onions, thinly sliced
- lemon zest, grated, 2 tablespoons
- 1 cup olives, pitted and sliced
- Salt and Ground black pepper
- 3 garlic cloves, crushed
- ½ teaspoon ground ginger
- ¼ teaspoon saffron threads, crushed
- 1½ cups of chicken broth
- fresh parsley leaves, chopped, ¼ cup
- fresh cilantro leaves, chopped, ¼ cup

INSTRUCTIONS:

1. Add salt and black pepper to the chicken and then drizzle lemon juice over it.
2. Heat the oil in a Dutch oven over high heat, then sear the chicken for 5 minutes on each side.
3. Except for the herbs, bring the remaining components to a boil.
4. Lower the heat to medium-low, and simmer for about 1 hour and 15 minutes.
5. Add the spices and herbs and simmer for an additional 15 minutes.

Egg Noodles with Croutons

Makes: 4

NUTRITION: Calories 565.3, Fat 27.2g, Sodium 145.0mg, Carbohydrates 67.3g, Protein 13.3g

INGREDIENTS:

- 12 ounces egg noodles, cooked
- Pinch Low-Sodium Salt
- ½ cup unsalted butter
- ¼ teaspoon pepper
- 2 slices of white bread, torn

INSTRUCTIONS:

1. Toast the bread slices in a skillet with hot butter until they are crisp.
2. Top with salt and pepper.
3. In a serving dish, mix the noodles and croutons and enjoy.

Roasted Balsamic Chicken

Makes: 4

NUTRITION: 182 Calories | 7 g Fat (2 g Saturated Fat) | 4g Carbohydrates | 25g Protein | 131mg Sodium

INGREDIENTS:

- black pepper, freshly ground
- 1 chicken (whole) chopped into pieces
- 2 tablespoons mustard (Dijon)
- olive oil, 2 tablespoons
- chicken broth, as required
- balsamic vinegar, 1 tablespoon
- freshly squeezed lemon juice, 2 tablespoons
- fresh parsley leaves 1 tablespoon
- lemon zest, 1 teaspoon
- 2 pressed garlic cloves
- Salt, 1 tablespoon

INSTRUCTIONS:

1. Preheat the oven to 400 degrees Fahrenheit.
2. Whisk the vinegar, mustard, lemon juice, garlic, olive oil, salt, and pepper.
3. In a resealable plastic bag, toss the dressing and the chicken pieces to coat.
4. Refrigerate for at least 2 hours, rotating occasionally.
5. Place chicken in an oiled casserole dish and bake for 1 hour.
6. Place the chicken on a serving plate.
7. Stir the chicken broth into the pan drippings.
8. Drizzle the juices over the chicken.
9. Serve the chicken with lemon zest and parsley garnish.

Turmeric Roasted Cauliflower

Makes: 5

NUTRITION: 124 Calories| Protein 3.5g| Carbohydrates 9.6 g | Fat 8.9g | Saturated Fat 1.4g | Sodium 554mg

INGREDIENTS:

- 8 cups cauliflower florets
- olive oil, 3 tablespoons
- cumin powder, ½ teaspoon
- lemon juice, 2 teaspoons
- black pepper, ½ teaspoon
- Salt, ½ teaspoon
- turmeric powder, 2 teaspoons
- 2 large garlic cloves, crushed

INSTRUCTIONS:

1. Turn up the oven's temperature to 425 F.
2. In a dish, combine the oil, salt, pepper, turmeric, cumin, and garlic.
3. Add the broccoli and set it on a baking sheet with a rim.
4. Roast until it's soft and golden.
5. Squeeze the lemon juice over the dish and then serve.

Fish Stew with Chili

Makes: 4

NUTRITION: 197 Calories| Protein 7.8g| Carbohydrates 24.2g | Fat 8.3g | Saturated Fat 4.3g|Sodium 41 Mg

INGREDIENTS:

- 2 fennel bulbs, chopped
- Ground fennel seeds, 1 teaspoon
- 3 bay leaves
- 1 red chili, finely chopped
- 1 tin plum tomatoes
- 6 tablespoons olive oil
- 2 cloves of garlic, crushed
- 1 lb. white fish fillet
- 3 ounces toasted almonds, ground
- 3 ounces of vegetable stock
- 1 onion, chopped
- sweet paprika powder, ½ teaspoon
- fresh thyme leaves, 1 tablespoon
- saffron strands, 1 teaspoon
- Quinoa and spring greens
- 1 lemon, cut into wedges

INSTRUCTIONS:

1. Steam onions, fennel, chili, crushed fennel seeds, and garlic.
2. Add paprika, thyme, saffron, bay leaves, and tomatoes.
3. Bring to a simmer with the vegetable stock.
4. Add the fish/tofu to the stew, along with the almonds.
5. Serve with greens, quinoa, and lemon wedges.

Fall Pumpkin Soup

Makes: 6

NUTRITION: Calories: 189cal | Carbohydrates: 22g | Protein: 3g | Fat: 11g | Saturated Fat: 6g | Sodium: 723mg

INGREDIENTS:

- 2½ cups pumpkin, peeled and sliced or diced
- vegetable broth, 2 cups
- cumin powder, 1 teaspoon
- ½ cup coconut milk
- frying oil
- 1 tablespoon lemongrass, chopped
- 1 ginger, peeled and grated
- 2 kaffir lime leaves, chopped
- 1 pinch of Black pepper
- 1 teaspoon coriander seeds
- 1 red pepper, seeded and sliced
- 1 fresh turmeric, peeled and sliced
- 1 shallot, chopped
- 4 garlic cloves

INSTRUCTIONS:

1. The squash should be tossed in the oil before being put on a baking pan and roasted until golden brown.
2. Heat the oil in a pan and cook the onions until they are browned.
3. Add the cilantro and cumin.
4. Include the kaffir leaves, turmeric, ginger, lemongrass, and chili, cooking for an additional minute while tossing.
5. Include the zucchini in the broth, cover, and then simmer for an additional ten minutes.
6. After adding the coconut milk, simmer for 6 minutes.

Bok choy and Orange duck

Makes: 6

NUTRITION: Calories: 337| Fat: 12.6g | Carbs: 14.2g | Protein: 31g

INGREDIENTS:

- 1½ pounds cooked duck meat, chopped
- orange zest, grated, 1 tablespoon
- fresh ginger, grated, 2 teaspoons
- ¼ cup chicken or vegetable broth
- ⅔ cup orange juice
- 3 pounds bok choi leaves
- 2 tablespoons coconut oil
- 1 orange, halved
- 1 onion, diced
- 2 garlic cloves, crushed

INSTRUCTIONS:

1. Melt the coconut oil in a pan over medium-high heat, then cook the onion, ginger, and garlic for about 3 minutes.
2. Add the orange juice, citrus zest, and broth, and bring to a rolling boil.
3. Add the duck flesh then cook for an additional three minutes. Set aside.
4. Add the pak choy to the same pan and sauté for 3 to 4 minutes.
5. Distribute the pak choi mixture among serving plates, then top with duck flesh.
6. Add orange slices as a garnish.

Pressed Lamb With Peas

Makes: 5

NUTRITION: Calories: 226| Fat: 9.7g | Carbs: 6.4g | Protein: 27.2g

INGREDIENTS:

- 3 dried red chilies
- 1 cinnamon stick
- 2 bay leaves
- 1-pound lean ground lamb
- ½ cup Roma tomatoes, chopped
- 4 garlic cloves, crushed
- ground coriander, 1½ teaspoons
- fresh cilantro, chopped, ¼ cup
- Salt and ground black pepper
- ground turmeric, ½ teaspoon
- ground cumin, ½ teaspoon

- ground nutmeg, ¼ teaspoon
- 1½ cups of water
- 3 green cardamom pods
- ½ teaspoon cumin
- ½ cup shelled fresh peas
- 1 medium red onion, diced
- 1-piece ginger, chopped
- 2 tablespoons plain yogurt, whipped
- 1 tablespoon coconut oil
- ½ teaspoon garam masala powder

INSTRUCTIONS:

1. In a Dutch oven, heat the oil over high heat while you sauté the onion for three to four minutes.
2. Add and sauté ginger, garlic, ground seasonings, and bay leaf for 1 minute.
3. Add and cook the beef for an additional five minutes.
4. Add tomatoes, and cook for about 10 minutes while turning occasionally.
5. Add water and green peas, then simmer on low for 25 to 30 minutes.
6. Cook for 4 to 5 minutes while stirring in the yogurt, parsley, salt, and black pepper.

CHAPTER 9
SNACKS AND SMOOTHIES

Easy Blueberry Muffins

Makes: 6

NUTRITION: Calories: 470| Fat: 35.4g | Carbohydrates: 26.8g | Protein: 12.6g

INGREDIENTS:

- almond flour, 2½ cups
- ¼ cup maple syrup
- 1 tablespoon organic vanilla extract
- coconut milk, ¼ cup
- coconut flour, 1 tablespoon

- baking soda, ½ teaspoon
- 3 tablespoons ground cinnamon
- Pinch of salt
- 2 organic eggs
- ¼ cup almond oil
- 1 cup fresh blueberries

INSTRUCTIONS:

1. Oil a muffin tin and preheat your oven to 350°F.
2. Combine the dry ingredients in a bowl, including the salt, baking soda, flour, and 2 teaspoons of cinnamon.
3. Combine the milk, oil, maple syrup, and vanilla essence in a separate bowl with the eggs.
4. Stir the flour mixture and egg combination together.
5. Add the blueberries.
6. Evenly distribute the ingredients into the muffin tins before adding the cinnamon.
7. Bake for roughly 24 minutes.

Olive Pizza bombs

Makes: 2

NUTRITION: 110 Calories|5g Fats|3g Carbohydrates|3g Protein

INGREDIENTS:

- 4 ounces of cream Cheese
- 4 slices Pepperoni, diced

- 4 pitted Black Olives, diced
- 2 tablespoons Sun-Dried Tomato Pesto

INSTRUCTIONS:

1. Combine basil, tomato pesto, and cream cheese in a mixing bowl.
2. Mix in the olives and pepperoni.
3. Form into balls and garnish with pepperoni, basil, and olives.

Cocoa peanut butter bombs

Makes: 8

NUTRITION: 207 Calories|20g Fats|0.8g Carbohydrates|4g Protein

INGREDIENTS:

- 2 tablespoons PB Fit Powder
- ¼ cup Cocoa Powder
- 2 tablespoons Shelled Hemp Seeds
- 28 drops of Liquid Stevia
- 2 tablespoons Heavy Cream
- Vanilla Extract, 1 teaspoon
- Coconut Oil, ½ cup
- ¼ cup Unsweetened Shredded Coconut

INSTRUCTIONS:

1. Mix the dry ingredients with the coconut oil.
2. Combine the heavy cream, vanilla, and liquid stevia in a mixing bowl. Remix until everything is well incorporated and the texture is somewhat creamy.
3. On a plate, pour unsweetened shredded coconut
4. Roll the balls in your palm, then roll them in coconut.
5. Place on a baking sheet with parchment paper and refrigerate for 20 minutes.

Jalapeño popper bombs

Makes: 2

NUTRITION: 200 Calories|13g Fats|5g Net Carb| 8g Protein

INGREDIENTS:

- ¼ teaspoon Onion Powder
- Garlic Powder, ¼ teaspoon
- ½ teaspoon Dried Parsley
- 3 ounces cream Cheese
- 3 slices Bacon, cooked crisp
- Salt and Pepper to Taste
- 1 Jalapeño Pepper, sliced

INSTRUCTIONS:

1. Mix the cream cheese, jalapeño, spices, salt, and pepper.
2. Stir in the bacon fat until it is firm.
3. Place crumbled bacon on a platter.
4. Form into balls, then roll the balls in bacon.

Low-Carb pan pizza dip

Makes: 1

NUTRITION: 349 Calories|35g Fats|4g Carbohydrates|14g Protein

INGREDIENTS:

- 6 ounces of cream cheese microwaved
- ½ cup Low-Carb Tomato Sauce
- ¼ cup Parmesan Cheese
- Sour Cream, ¼ cup
- Salt and Pepper to Taste
- ¼ cup Mayonnaise
- Mozzarella Cheese, shredded, ½ cup
- ½ cup Mozzarella Cheese, shredded

INSTRUCTIONS:

1. Turn up the oven's temperature to 350°F.
2. Combine the mozzarella, cream cheese, sour cream, mayonnaise, salt, and pepper.
3. Pour into ramekins and spread Tomato Sauce over each ramekin as well as mozzarella cheese and parmesan cheese.
4. Top your pan pizza dips with your favorite toppings.
5. Bake for 20 minutes.
6. Serve alongside some tasty breadsticks or pork rinds!

Apple, beet, and strawberry smoothie

Makes: 2

NUTRITION: Calories: 400| Fat: 29.2g | Carbs: 36.7g | Protein: 1.7g

INGREDIENTS:

- 3 Medjool dates, pitted and chopped
- 1 cup frozen strawberries, peeled and sliced
- 1 beetroot, peeled and sliced or diced
- 1 cup apple, peeled, cored, and sliced
- ¼ cup extra-virgin coconut oil
- ½ cup almond milk, unsweetened

INSTRUCTIONS:

1. Combine everything and process until it's smooth.
2. Distribute the smoothie among the two cups.

Pizza Breadsticks

Makes: 4

NUTRITION: Calories 722 Fat 39.1 g, Carbohydrates 66.6g, Protein 29.2 g, Sodium 1027 mg

INGREDIENTS:

BREADSTICK BASE
• Mozzarella Cheese, melted, 2 cups
• Almond Flour, ¾ cup
• Psyllium Husk Powder, 1 tablespoon
• Cream Cheese, 3 tablespoons
• 1 Egg
• Baking Powder, 1 teaspoon
• Italian Seasoning, 2 tablespoons

• Salt, 1 teaspoon
• Pepper, 1 teaspoon

TOPPINGS
• garlic powder, 1 teaspoon
• Cheddar Cheese, 3 ounces
• Onion Powder, 1 teaspoon
• Parmesan Cheese, ¼ cup

INSTRUCTIONS:

1. Turn the oven's temperature up to 400 degrees.
2. Combine the cream cheese and egg.
3. Combine the dry components in a different bowl.
4. Combine the mozzarella cheese with the wet and dry components.
5. Use your palms to combine the dough. Place a Silpat down.
6. Place the dough on foil so you can use a pizza cutter to shape it.
7. Cut the dough into segments and sprinkle salt and pepper over it.
8. Bake for 14 minutes, or until golden.

Chickpea and flax seed tortillas

Makes: 10

NUTRITION: Calories: 80 | Fat: 2 g | Saturated Fat: 0g | Carbohydrates: 11.7g | Protein: 4g|Sodium 110 mg

INGREDIENTS:

• 2 tablespoons lukewarm water
• 1 cup chickpea flour
• 2 tablespoons ground flax seeds

• 1 cup of water
• Pinch of sea salt, turmeric, cumin
• Olive oil is too runny

INSTRUCTIONS:

1. In a dish, mix lukewarm water and flax seeds.
2. Allow to coagulate for 5 to 10 minutes.
3. Add one-half cup of the mixture to a pan and stir to cover the bottom.
4. Cook for 3 minutes or so.
5. Flip and heat for an additional 1 minute.

Crusty Peanut butter bars

Makes: 2

NUTRITION: Calories 795.6, Fat 37.6 g, Sodium 1842.2 mg, Carbohydrates 73.2, Protein 41.2 g

INGREDIENTS:

CRUST
- ½ teaspoon Cinnamon
- 1 tablespoon Erythritol
- Pinch of Salt
- 1 cup Almond Flour
- ¼ cup butter melted

FUDGE
- ¼ cup Erythritol

- ½ cup Peanut Butter
- ¼ cup Heavy Cream
- ⅛ teaspoon Xanthan Gum
- ¼ cup butter melted
- Vanilla Extract, ½ teaspoon

TOPPING
- ⅓ cup Chocolate, Chopped

INSTRUCTIONS:

1. Turn the oven temperature to 400 degrees Fahrenheit.
2. Mix almond flour with half of the melted butter followed by erythritol and cinnamon.
3. Press into a baking tray that has been lined, and bake for 10 minutes.
4. Blend all of the fudge ingredients and spread up the sides of the baking dish.
5. Top your bars with chopped chocolate just before cooling.
6. Remove the bars by peeling the parchment paper out once they have cooled.

Grape Berry Smoothie

Makes: 2

NUTRITION: Calories: 251|Fat: 4g|Carbohydrates: 53g |Protein: 19g|Sodium 11 mg

INGREDIENTS:

- 2 cups fresh baby spinach, stems removed and chopped
- seedless green grapes, ½ cup
- cinnamon powder, 1 teaspoon

- chia seeds, 2 tablespoons
- Raspberries, 1 cup
- 1 Medjool date (soften/soaked)
- ½ cup of water

INSTRUCTIONS:

1. Pour all the components into a blender, excluding the distilled water.
2. Add water to desired consistency. Process until smooth

Carrot and Onion muffins

Makes: 5

NUTRITION: Calories: 590| Fat: 49.3g | Carbohydrates: 21.9g | Protein: 17.5g | Sodium: 31mg

INGREDIENTS:

- almond flour, ¾ cup
- apple cider vinegar, 2 teaspoons
- 2 carrots, peeled and grated
- fresh parsley, chopped, ½ cup
- almond oil, melted, 2 tablespoons
- fresh dill, chopped, 2 teaspoons
- Pinch of salt
- 4 organic eggs
- whey protein powder, ¼ cup
- lemon juice, 3 tablespoons
- baking soda, ½ teaspoon
- coconut butter, softened, 1 cup
- 1 bunch of spring onions, chopped

INSTRUCTIONS:

1. Set your oven to 350 degrees Fahrenheit and grease a muffin pan.
2. Combine the flour, baking soda, protein powder, and salt.
3. In a separate dish, mix the eggs, vinegar, lemon juice, and oil.
4. Include the coconut butter and whisk the combination until it is smooth.
5. Combine the flour mixture with the egg combination.
6. Add the parsley, carrots, and spring onions.
7. Scoop the batter into the muffin tins, then bake for 20 minutes.
8. Place the warm muffins on a serving dish after inverting them.

Watercress Cranberry Smoothie

Makes: 2

NUTRITION: Calories 198|Fat 1g|Carbohydrates 47g|Protein 5g | Sodium18mg

INGREDIENTS:

- 2 cups watercress
- 1 cup of pineapple
- 1 ripe banana, sliced
- 1 orange, peeled and sliced or diced
- 1 pitted Medjool date (optional)
- 1 tablespoon powdered wheatgrass
- Purified water

INSTRUCTIONS:

1. Pour all the components into a blender, excluding the distilled water.
2. Add water for desired consistency.
3. Process until smooth.

Neapolitan bombs

Makes: 24

NUTRITION: 102 Calories |9g Fats | 0.4g Carbohydrates | 0.6g Protein, | 23.1mg Sodium

INGREDIENTS:

- ½ cup butter
- ½ cup Sour Cream
- Cocoa Powder, 2 tablespoons
- ½ cup Coconut Oil
- 2 Strawberries
- Liquid Stevia, 25 drops
- ½ cup Cream Cheese
- 2 tablespoons Erythritol
- Vanilla Extract, 1 teaspoon

INSTRUCTIONS:

1. Use an immersion mixer to thoroughly combine the butter, coconut oil, sour cream, cream cheese, erythritol, and stevia.
2. The mixture should be divided into three containers. Put the strawberries in one dish, the vanilla in another, and the cocoa powder in a third.
3. Pour the chocolate mixture midway into a fat bomb mold. Freeze for 30 minutes.
4. Continue with the vanilla mixture, and freeze for 30 minutes.
5. Finish with the strawberry mixture and freeze again.
6. Once they have hardened, take them out of the fat bomb molds.

Freekeh balls

Makes: 25

NUTRITION: 290 calories | 9g Fat | 3.5g saturated fat | 38g Carbohydrates | 13g protein | 25mg Sodium

INGREDIENTS:

- 1 cup uncooked crushed freekeh
- 1 onion, grated
- 2 ½ cups of water
- 1 potato, grated
- 2 garlic cloves, crushed
- ½ cup parsley, chopped
- ¾ cup plain or Italian breadcrumbs
- ¾ cup Pecorino Romano cheese, grated
- 3 eggs, beaten
- ¼ teaspoon black pepper
- 2 tablespoons olive oil for brushing
- ½ teaspoon of salt

INSTRUCTIONS:

1. Turn the oven's temperature up to 400 degrees.
2. Line two baking sheets with parchment paper.
3. Combine water and freekeh in a pot.
4. Bring to a boil, then reduce the heat and cook for 20 minutes.
5. Once the freekeh has cooled somewhat, mix everything (aside from the olive oil) and chill for at least an hour.
6. Place 1 heaping tablespoon of the mixture between your palms and carefully roll it into a meatball.
7. Place 13 meatballs on each cookie tray with a liner.
8. Turn over using a heat-resistant spatula, then bake for 10 minutes, or until golden brown.

Cherry and kale smoothie

Makes: 2

NUTRITION: Calories: 187| Fat: 1.7g | Carbs: 44.2g | Protein: 4.2g

INGREDIENTS:

- 2 ripe bananas, peeled and sliced
- fresh cherries, pitted, 1 cup
- fresh kale, trimmed, 1 cup
- 1 teaspoon fresh ginger, peeled, and sliced or diced
- 1 cup coconut water
- 1 tablespoon chia seeds, soaked for 15 minutes
- ½ teaspoon ground turmeric
- ¼ teaspoon ground cinnamon

INSTRUCTIONS:

1. Place all components in a powerful blender and blend until well combined.
2. Immediately serve the smoothie in two cups.

Corndog Muffins

Makes: 10

NUTRITION: 77 Calories | 8g Fats | 0.7g Carbohydrates
| 4.1g Protein | 438.9mg Sodium

INGREDIENTS:

- 3 tablespoons Swerve Sweetener
- ½ cup Blanched Almond Flour
- ½ cup Flaxseed Meal
- melted butter, ¼ cup
- 10 Smokies, halved
- ¼ teaspoon Low-Sodium Salt

- 1 tablespoon Psyllium Husk Powder
- 1 Egg
- ⅓ cup Sour Cream
- ¼ teaspoon Baking Powder
- ¼ cup Coconut Milk

INSTRUCTIONS:

1. Turn up the oven's temperature to 375 F.
2. Combine each dry component.
3. Add the egg, sour cream, and butter and mix well.
4. Add the coconut milk and stir.
5. Smokies should be positioned in the batter's middle.
6. Bake for 12 minutes, followed by 2 minutes of broiling.
7. Leave the muffins in the pan to settle for a few minutes before transferring them to a wire rack to finish cooling.
8. Garnish with spring onions when serving.

Cheddar and Bell pepper pizza

Makes: 2

NUTRITION: 410 Calories | 33g Fats | 3g Carbohydrates
| 28g Protein | 601mg Sodium

INGREDIENTS:

- Tomato Sauce, ¼ cup
- Diced Bell Peppers, ⅔ cup
- Pizza dough

- Shredded Cheddar Cheese, 4 ounces
- Tomato, 1 Vine
- Fresh Basil, 2-3 tablespoons

INSTRUCTIONS:

1. Turn the oven temperature up to 350ºF.
2. Bake the dough for about 8 minutes.
3. Slice vine tomato and place on each pizza dough, along with 2 tablespoons tomato sauce.
4. Top with shredded Cheddar cheese and bell peppers and bake for another 10 minutes.
5. Serve garnished with fresh basil.

Fried Queso Blanco

Makes: 1

NUTRITION: 520 Calories | 43g Fats | 2g Carbohydrates | 30g Protein | 170mg Sodium

INGREDIENTS:

- Queso Blanco cubed, 6 ounces
- 1 Pinch Red Pepper Flakes
- Olive Oil, 1½ tablespoons
- Olives, 2 ounces

INSTRUCTIONS:

1. Heat the oil and melt the cheese cubes.
2. Continue to heat the cheese, then fold half of it in on itself.
3. Continue to flip the cheese and heat it until a beautiful crust forms.
4. Use the melted cheese to form a cube, sealing the edges with a second spatula.
5. Turn off the heat.
6. Cut into pieces and serve with pepper flakes and olive oil.

Ham and Cheese Stromboli

Makes: 4

NUTRITION: 300 Calories | 28g Fats | 7g Carbohydrates | 26g Protein | 902mg Sodium

INGREDIENTS:

- Almond Flour, 4 tablespoons
- Coconut Flour, 3 tablespoons
- 2 cups Mozzarella Cheese, shredded
- Salt and Pepper to Taste
- 1 Egg
- 5 ounces of Cheddar Cheese
- 4 ounces Ham
- Italian Seasoning, 1 teaspoon

INSTRUCTIONS:

1. Mix almond, coconut flour, and seasonings.
2. Start incorporating the melted mozzarella into your flour mixture.
3. Add your egg and stir everything together.
4. Transfer the dough to parchment paper and place another parchment paper on top; flatten it out with a rolling pin.
5. Cut diagonal lines from the edges of the dough to the center with a pizza cutter.
6. Alternate between ham and cheddar on the uncut dough stretch.
7. Then, one slice of dough at a time, lift it and place it on top of the filling, covering it completely.
8. Bake for 20 minutes.

Mini Portobello pizzas

Makes: 4

NUTRITION: 320 Calories | 31g Fats | 8g Carbohydrates | 5g Protein | 670mg Sodium

INGREDIENTS:

- 1 Vine Tomato, sliced thin
- ¼ Cup Fresh Chopped Basil
- Pinch Low-Sodium Salt and Pepper
- 4 ounces of mozzarella Cheese
- 20 slices Pepperoni
- 6 tablespoons Olive Oil
- 4 Portobello Mushroom Caps

INSTRUCTIONS:

1. Scrape out all of the mushroom's insides.
2. Preheat the oven to high broil and brush the insides of the mushrooms with Olive Oil. Season with salt and pepper.
3. Broil the mushroom for 3 minutes.
4. Brush olive oil on the mushrooms' undersides and season them with salt and pepper.
5. Broil a further 4 minutes.
6. In each mushroom, place a tomato and basil leaf.
7. Top each mushroom with 5 pieces of pepperoni and fresh cubed mozzarella cheese.
8. Broil for another 2 minutes.

Berry Cleanser Smoothie

Makes: 2

NUTRITION: Calories 202.4 |Fat 4.5 g | Saturated Fat 2.3 g
|Sodium 36.5 mg| Carbohydrate 33 g| Protein 13 g

INGREDIENTS:

- 3 Swiss chard leaves, stems removed
- ¼ cup frozen cranberries
- Water, 1 cup

- 1 cup of raspberries
- 2 pitted Medjool date
- 2 tablespoons ground flaxseed

INSTRUCTIONS:

1. Add all the ingredients and blend till smooth.

Sweet Potato Chicken Dumplings

Makes: 8

NUTRITION: 188 Calories|4g Fat|1g Saturated|18mg Sodium
|29g Carbohydrates|13g Protein

INGREDIENTS:

- frozen peas, 1 cup
- all-purpose flour, divided, ½ cup
- cooked chicken breast, shredded, 3 cups
- carrots, sliced, 1 cup
- 2 cloves garlic, pressed
- baking soda, 1 teaspoon
- low-sodium chicken broth, 2 cups
- black pepper, divided, 1 teaspoon

- kale, stemmed and chopped, 1 cup
- wheat flour, 1 cup
- 1 onion, chopped
- olive oil, 1 tablespoon
- Buttermilk, 1 cup
- green beans, halved, 1 cup
- 1 sweet potato, cooked, peeled, and mashed
- Low-Sodium Salt, ⅛ teaspoon

INSTRUCTIONS:

1. Heat the oil in a pan.
2. For 8 minutes, sauté shallots with carrots, green beans, peas, kale, garlic, and pepper.
3. Add the flour and cook for an additional three minutes.
4. Add broth and then bring the liquid to a boil.
5. Combine the shredded poultry with the vegetables.
6. Distribute the mixture equally among the 16 muffin tins.
7. Combine the leftover pepper, salt, baking soda, and flour in a mixing bowl.
8. Add the buttermilk and the pureed sweet potato.
9. Top with the poultry mixture in the muffin cups.
10. Bake for 15 minutes, or until browned.

CHAPTER 10
VEGAN

Tofu and vegetable skewers

Makes: 4

NUTRITION: 353 calories| 24g of protein | 18g fat (3g saturated) | 28g of carbohydrates

INGREDIENTS:

- 1-pound extra-firm tofu squeezed dry and cubed
- zest and juice of 1 lime
- 16 mushrooms
- 16 bunches of broccoli
- 2 tablespoons olive oil
- 1 tablespoon garlic, crushed
- 1 zucchini, sliced
- 2 onions, sliced
- ⅓ cup vegetable broth or water
- 2 tablespoons agave nectar or maple syrup
- 1½ tablespoons of tamari
- 1 teaspoon hot sauce
- 2 bell peppers, diced
- grated ginger, 1 tablespoon
- black pepper, ¼ teaspoon
- curry powder, 1 Tablespoon

INSTRUCTIONS:

1. Thread each skewer in this order: a mushroom, a piece of orange pepper, a broccoli floret, a cube of tofu, a slice of zucchini, a piece of red pepper, and a new onion. Repeat the process, reversing the order and ending with a mushroom.
2. Layer skewers in a baking dish.
3. For the marinade, place the broth, oil, agave nectar, lime zest and juice, tamari, curry powder, garlic, ginger, hot sauce, and pepper in a bowl and whisk together.
4. Pour marinade over skewers.
5. Cover the mold, place it in the refrigerator, and let the tofu and vegetables marinate for 1 hour or more.
6. Grill the skewers on a hot oiled grill or griddle until the tofu and vegetables are lightly charred, 3 minutes per side.

Snow peas, Pine nuts & Asparagus Salad

Makes: 2

NUTRITION: Calories 239| Fat 22g | Carbohydrate 7g| Protein 7g

INGREDIENTS:

- ½ packet of fresh bean sprouts
- A sprinkling of pine nuts
- snow peas, 2 cups
- Spinach, 1 cup
- Cold-pressed olive oil
- asparagus, 1 bunch

INSTRUCTIONS:

1. Steam the asparagus and snow peas on medium heat for 3 to 6 minutes.
2. Add a dash of salt and pepper to the asparagus and snow peas.
3. Pour lemon juice directly over the lettuce.

Vegan Rice Paper Rolls

Makes: 2

NUTRITION: 197 Calories| Protein 7.8g| Carbohydrates 24.2g | Sugar 3.1 g | Fat 8.3g | Saturated Fat 4.3g

INGREDIENTS:

- ½ cucumber cut into matchsticks
- A handful of bean sprouts
- Uncooked Rice paper
- 4 spring onions
- A handful of coriander, chopped
- 1 carrot, cut into matchsticks
- Liquid Aminos
- 1 chili

INSTRUCTIONS:

1. Cook the rice paper rolls by soaking them in a big bowl of boiling water until they become flexible.
2. Toss the coriander with the other ingredients in the rice paper wrappers.
3. Roll and dress in Liquid Aminos.

Asian-Italian Tofu and Capers Pizza

Makes: 4

NUTRITION: Calories 796, Fat 38 g, Sodium 1842 mg, Carbohydrates 73, Protein 41 g

INGREDIENTS:

- 14.5-ounce can of diced tomatoes, drained
- 2 tablespoons olive oil
- 16-ounce package of tofu drained and sliced
- Pinch Salt
- 3 garlic cloves, pressed
- ¼ cup sun-dried tomatoes, sliced
- Sugar, ½ teaspoon
- Capers, 1 tablespoon
- dried oregano, 1 teaspoon
- fresh parsley, 2 tablespoon
- Freshly cracked black pepper

INSTRUCTIONS:

1. Turn up the oven's temperature to 275°F.
2. In an oiled pan, cook the tofu until it turns golden.
3. Add salt and pepper for seasoning.
4. Sauté the garlic for one minute in the heated residual oil.
5. Add tomato, olive, and caper.
6. Add the oregano, sugar, and salt before adding pepper to taste.
7. Cook for approximately ten minutes.
8. Pour the sauce over the tofu pieces that have been fried and decorate them with parsley.

Asian Edamame & Tofu Bowl

Makes: 4

NUTRITION: Calories: 167|Fat: 5g|Saturated: 1g|Carbohydrate: 23g |Protein: 6g

INGREDIENTS:

- 1 yellow onion, pressed
- 4 shiitake mushroom caps, sliced
- 2 green onions, chopped small
- 10 ounces firm tofu, crumbled
- grated fresh ginger, 1 teaspoon
- toasted sesame oil, 1 tablespoon
- 1 cup shelled edamame, cooked in salted water
- toasted sesame seeds, 1 tablespoon
- soy sauce, 2 tablespoons
- Cooked brown rice, 3 cups
- canola oil, 1 tablespoon

INSTRUCTIONS:

1. In a pan, heat the canola oil. Sauté the onion for about 5 minutes.
2. Include the mushrooms and simmer for an additional 5 minutes.
3. Include the green scallions and ginger.
4. Add the tofu, soy sauce, and ginger, and cook for about five minutes.
5. Include the edamame and stir regularly while cooking.
6. Divide the hot rice among four plates, then top each with the tofu, edamame, and sesame oil mixture.
7. Serve with sesame seeds as a topping.

Asparagus and Zucchini Pasta

Makes: 4

NUTRITION: Calories 160| Fat 3g (Saturated 0g) | Sodium 549mg | Carbohydrate 30g| Protein 8g

INGREDIENTS:

- 1 zucchini
- 1 bunch of asparagus, steamed
- 4 tomatoes, diced
- 200g of rocket
- 12 basil leaves
- 2 cloves garlic
- ½ red onion, diced
- 4 servings of spelt pasta, cooked
- Olive oil

INSTRUCTIONS:

1. Combine onion and tomatoes with handfuls of rocket, and asparagus and set them aside.
2. Blend remaining ingredients until a smooth, light green sauce forms.
3. Toss the pasta with the sauce, divide it into bowls, and top with the tomato, red onion, asparagus, and rocket.

Tofu and Tomato Sloppy Joe

Makes: 4

NUTRITION: Calories: 209| Fat: 10 g | Carbohydrates: 21g | sugar: 13 g | Protein: 11g

INGREDIENTS:

- ¼ cup apple cider vinegar
- 1 onion, diced
- 10 ounces of tofu, chopped
- 2 cans (14 ounces) of tomato puree
- olive oil, 2 tablespoons
- chili powder, 1 tablespoon
- garlic powder, 1 teaspoon
- sea salt, ½ teaspoons
- black pepper, ⅛ teaspoon

INSTRUCTIONS:

1. In a big pot, heat the olive oil on medium-high heat.
2. Include tofu and scallion, and cook for approximately 5 minutes.
3. Add salt, pepper, chile powder, apple cider vinegar, and tomatoes to the mixture.
4. Simmer for 10 minutes, stirring occasionally to enable flavors to meld.

Thai Tempeh cabbage leaf rolls

Makes: 4

NUTRITION: 230 calories| 10g protein | 17g fat (2g saturated) | 10g carbohydrates

INGREDIENTS:

- 8 ounces of tempeh, sliced horizontally into 8 pieces
- 1 tablespoon of tamari
- 1⅓ cup sauerkraut, drained
- 2 tablespoons olive oil
- 6 tablespoons chipotle and almond mayonnaise
- 4 kale leaves, lower stems trimmed

INSTRUCTIONS:

1. On a plate, place the tempeh.
2. Drizzle the tempeh with the tamari and let stand for 10 minutes.
3. Cook the sauerkraut with a half-teaspoon of oil, stirring periodically, until it is crisp.
4. Cook the tempeh in the leftover oil in the same skillet for 5 minutes, flipping after 3 minutes.
5. To assemble each roll, place 1 cabbage leaf, ribs side up, on a cutting board.
6. Spread 1½ tablespoons of chipotle and almond mayonnaise in the center of the sheet.
7. Top the mayonnaise with 2 pieces of tempeh, ⅓ cup of sauerkraut, and 1 slice of cucumber.
8. Fold the end of the stem and the top edge of the cabbage leaf towards the center.
9. Fold the right side tightly over the filling, then fold and overlap the left side of the sheet.

Bowl of fruit and Vegan yogurt

Makes: 2

NUTRITION: Calories: 87 | Fat: 5.1g | Carbohydrates: 30.5g | Sugars: 17g | Protein: 7.6g

INGREDIENTS:

- 1 cup plant-based yogurt
- 2 tablespoons of polaner sugar
- ¼ teaspoon ground cinnamon
- Strawberries, ½ cup, peeled and sliced
- Blueberries, ¼ cup
- Raspberries, ½ cup
- 2 tablespoons almonds, chopped

INSTRUCTIONS:

1. Put the yogurt, sugar, and cinnamon in a bowl and stir.
2. Divide the yogurt into serving bowls.
3. Garnish with berries and nuts and serve immediately.

Quinoa with pineapple

Makes: 4

NUTRITION: Calories: 413 | Carbs: 56g | Protein: 13g | Lipids: 16g | Saturated Fat: 7g

INGREDIENTS:

FOR THE TOFU:
- Tofu triangles
- 10 small triangles of tofu
- 1 tablespoon of maple syrup
- 2 teaspoons tamari
- ½ cup onion, diced
- 1 cup shiitake mushrooms, sliced
- black pepper, ground

FOR THE PINEAPPLE AND QUINOA:
- 1 ½ cups fresh pineapple, diced
- 4 cups cooked quinoa
- ¼ red onion, diced
- sautéed shiitake + onion in a pan of tofu

- 1 cup kale
- ½ teaspoon dried jalapeno
- a touch of salt
- a dash of maple syrup
- ¼ cup nutritional yeast

PINEAPPLE TAHINI VINAIGRETTE
- pineapple juice, 3 tablespoons
- Tahini, 2 tablespoons
- chopped mint, 1 teaspoon

FOR GARNISH:
- Pineapple, ½ cup, finely diced
- Safflower oil for frying
- mint, 1 tablespoon, chopped

INSTRUCTIONS:

FOR THE TOFU:
1. Start by applying a light coating of safflower oil.
2. Add the pieces of tofu and simmer for approximately one minute.
3. Add the tamari and maple syrup after that, along with plenty of freshly ground black pepper.
4. Cooking time should be 2 minutes per side.
5. Add the shiitake mushrooms and shallots after that.
6. Cook the veggies for 15 minutes or until they are tender.
7. After taking the tofu from the pan, set it aside.

FOR THE PINEAPPLE AND QUINOA:
8. To the skillet, add the quinoa, pineapple, red onion, mint, kale, nutritional yeast, and jalapeno.
9. Drizzle with safflower oil as well.
10. Cook the quinoa for about 3 minutes, turning it to ensure even cooking.

FOR GARNISH:
11. Sauté the garnish ingredients. Set apart.

TO SERVE:
12. Place the cooked quinoa on the serving dish, then add the pineapple as a topping.
13. Serve with tofu and dressing on the side.

Barley vegetable soup

Makes: 6

NUTRITION: Calories: 277.37|Carbohydrates: 52.82g|Protein: 7.43g
|Fats: 5.9g

INGREDIENTS:

- 15-ounce can of beans, drained and rinsed
- 1 cup carrots, chopped
- vegetable broth, 4 cups
- 1 clove of garlic, pressed
- ¾ cup peeled barley

- Vegan parmesan, Grated
- 1 cup celery, chopped
- 28-ounce can of tomato purée
- kale, coarsely chopped, 2 cups
- 1 sprig of rosemary

INSTRUCTIONS:

1. In a skillet, sauté the celery, onions, and carrots in olive oil.
2. Include the barley, thyme, and garlic.
3. Add vegetable broth and bring the broth to a boil while stirring continuously.
4. Lower the heat to a medium setting and simmer for about an hour before adding the tomatoes and beans.
5. Serve the dish with veggie parmesan sprinkled on top.

Fried rice with tofu and kale

Makes: 4

NUTRITION: Calories: 301| Fat: 11g | Carbohydrates: 36g | Protein: 16g

INGREDIENTS:

- kale, stemmed and chopped, 2 cups
- 2 tablespoons olive oil (extra-virgin)
- ¼ cup wok sauce

- 8 ounces of tofu, chopped
- cooked brown rice, 3 cups
- 6 spring onions, finely sliced

INSTRUCTIONS:

1. In a pan, warm the olive oil to a simmer over high heat.
2. Include broccoli, tofu, and green onions.
3. Cook, stirring frequently, for 5 to 7 minutes or until veggies are tender.
4. Stir in sauce and brown rice.
5. Heat thoroughly for 3 to 5 minutes while stirring periodically.

Tofu and spinach

Makes: 4

NUTRITION: Calories:128| Fat: 10 g | Carbohydrates: 7g | Protein: 6g

INGREDIENTS:

- 3 garlic cloves, crushed
- 1 onion, diced
- 4 cups fresh baby spinach
- 8 ounces of tofu

- juice of 1 orange
- zest of 1 orange
- olive oil, 2 tablespoons
- sea salt, ½ teaspoons
- black pepper, ⅛ teaspoon

INSTRUCTIONS:

1. In a pan over medium-high heat, warm the olive oil.
2. Combine the tofu, onion, and spinach in the pan.
3. Cook, stirring periodically, for approximately 5 minutes.
4. Add the crushed garlic cloves and sauté for 30 seconds.
5. Taste-test and add the orange juice, peel, salt, and pepper.
6. Cook, stirring periodically, for 3 minutes.

Tofu and red pepper

Makes: 4

NUTRITION: Calories: 166| Fat: 10 g | Carbohydrates: 17 g | sugar: 12g |Protein: 7g

INGREDIENTS:

- 1 onion, diced
- 1 serving of Ginger teriyaki sauce
- 2 bell peppers, diced

- tofu, chopped, 8 ounces
- olive oil, 2 tablespoons

INSTRUCTIONS:

1. In a pan over medium-high heat, warm the olive oil.
2. Add the tofu, onion, and bell pepper, and cook for 5 to 7 minutes, stirring periodically.
3. Fill the pan with the teriyaki sauce.
4. Cook the sauce for 3 to 4 minutes, swirling frequently, until it thickens.
5. Serve and enjoy!

CONCLUSION

For those looking to improve their diet, physical performance, and health, carb cycling may be a helpful aid. Here's how to get started if you believe carb cycling might be the correct choice for you. First and foremost, keeping note of your macros is crucial. The next step is to determine how many calories of carbohydrates you should consume daily. Body weight, age, sex, the intensity of your workouts, as well as paying attention to your body, and hunger signals, all play a significant role in this.

From a physiological and psychological standpoint, a mix of the two carbohydrate types may be preferable to a long-term low or high-carbohydrate diet. Consider consulting a dietitian if you want to find the right protocol and carbohydrate intake amounts that are ideal for you. Additionally, if you take any medications or have any medical conditions, such as diabetes, it's imperative to consult your doctor before making any dietary adjustments.

Happy Carb-Cycling!

MEASUREMENT CONVERSION CHART

TO CONVERT X » Y	1 OF THIS	EQUALS THIS
VOLUME TO WEIGHT		
tablespoons » teaspoons	1 tablespoon	3 teaspoons
tablespoons » fluid ounces	1 tablespoon	0.5 fluid ounces
tablespoons » sticks of butter	1 tablespoon	0.125 sticks of butter
tablespoons » cups	1 tablespoon	0.0625 cups
teaspoons » tablespoons	1 teaspoon	0.33 tablespoons
teaspoons » cups	1 teaspoon	0.02 cups
teaspoons » fluid ounces	1 teaspoon	0.16 fluid ounces
fluid ounces » tablespoons	1 fluid ounce	2 tablespoons
fluid ounces » teaspoons	1 fluid ounce	6 teaspoons
fluid ounces » cups	1 fluid ounce	0.125 cups
cups » fluid ounces	1 cup	8 fluid ounces
cups » tablespoons	1 cup	16 tablespoons
cups » teaspoons	1 cup	48 teaspoons
cups » pints	1 cup	0.5 pints
cups » quarts	1 cup	0.25 quarts
cups » gallons	1 cup	0.0625 gallons
pints » cups	1 pint	2 cups
quarts » pints	1 quart	2 pints
quarts » cups	1 quart	4 cups
gallon » quarts	1 gallon	4 quarts
gallon » cups	1 gallon	16 cups
pinch » teaspoons	1 pinch	0.1 teaspoons
dash » teaspoons	1 dash	0.2 teaspoons
cup dry beans » pounds	1 cup dry beans	0.4 pounds
cup butter » pounds	1 cup butter	0.5 pounds
cup choc. chips » ounces	1 cup chocolate chips	6 ounces
cup cheerios » ounces	1 cup cheerios	1.33 ounces
cup cocoa » ounces	1 cup cocoa	3 ounces
cup corn syrup » ounces	1 cup corn syrup	11.5 ounces
cup cornmeal » ounces	1 cup cornmeal	4.5 ounces
cup flour » ounces	1 cup flour	4 ounces
cup flour » pounds	1 cup flour	0.25 pounds
cup honey » pounds	1 cup honey	0.75 pounds
cup honey » ounces	1 cup honey	12 ounces

cup jam » ounces	1 cup jam	12 ounces
cup molasses » ounces	1 cup molasses	11.6 ounces
cup oats » ounces	1 cup oats	3.5 ounces
cup oats » pounds	1 cup oats	0.22 pounds
cup oil » ounces	1 cup oil	7.5 ounces
cup peanut butter » ounces	1 cup peanut butter	9.5 ounces
cup raisins » ounces	1 cup raisins	5.5 ounces
cup rice » ounces	1 cup rice	7 ounces
cup rice » pounds	1 cup rice	0.4375 pounds
cup rice flour » ounces	1 cup rice flour	4.5 ounces
cup shortening » ounces	1 cup shortening	7 ounces
cup sour cream » ounces	1 cup sour cream	8 ounces
cup sugar » ounces	1 cup sugar	7 ounces
cup sugar » pounds	1 cup sugar	0.4375 pounds
cup sugar (brown) » ounces	1 cup brown sugar	7.5 ounces
cup sugar (powdered) » ounces	1 cup powdered sugar	4 ounces
cup water » ounces	1 cup water	8.3 ounces
cup walnuts (chopped) » ounces	1 cup walnuts	4.3 ounces
cup wheat » pounds	1 cup wheat	0.48 pounds
cup dried milk (nonfat) » ounces	1 cup dried milk (nonfat)	3 ounces
egg (powdered) » ounces	1 egg (powdered)	0.5 ounces
egg (large) » fluid ounces	1 egg (large)	2 fluid ounces
egg white » teaspoons	1 egg white	8 teaspoons
egg white » cups	1 egg white	48 cups
egg yolk » teaspoons	1 egg yolk	4 teaspoons
stick butter » cups	1 stick butter	0.5 cups
stick butter » ounces	1 stick butter	4 ounces
stick butter » tablespoons	1 stick butter	8 tablespoons
tablespoons baking soda » ounces	1 tablespoon baking soda	0.5 ounces
tablespoons baking powder » ounces	1 tablespoon baking powder	0.5 ounces
tablespoons baking powder » pounds	1 tablespoon baking powder	0.03125 pounds
tablespoons cocoa » ounces	1 tablespoon cocoa	0.1875 ounces
tablespoons cocoa » pounds	1 tablespoon cocoa	0.01 pounds
tablespoons cornstarch » ounces	1 tablespoon cornstarch	0.33 ounces
tablespoons jam » ounces	1 tablespoon jam	0.75 ounces
tablespoons honey » ounces	1 tablespoon honey	0.75 ounces
tablespoons honey » pounds	1 tablespoon honey	0.0468 pounds
tablespoons oil » ounces	1 tablespoon oil	0.46875 ounces
tablespoons peanut butter » ounces	1 tablespoon peanut butter	0.59375 ounces

tablespoons salt » ounces	1 tablespoon salt	0.6 ounces
tablespoons shortening » ounces	1 tablespoon shortening	0.4375 ounces
tablespoons spices » ounces	1 tablespoon spices	0.25 ounces
tablespoons vinegar » ounces	1 tablespoon vinegar	0.5 ounces
tablespoons yeast » ounces	1 tablespoon yeast	0.5 ounces
tablespoons yeast » ounces	1 tablespoon yeast	0.33 ounces
teaspoons baking soda » ounces	1 teaspoon baking soda	0.16 ounces
teaspoons baking powder » ounces	1 teaspoon baking powder	0.16 ounces
teaspoons salt » ounces	1 teaspoon salt	0.2 ounces
pound flour » cups	1 pound flour	4 cups
pound sugar » cups	1 pound sugar	2.285 cups
ounces oats » cups	1-ounce oats	0.285 cups
Pound rice » cups	1 pound rice	2.285 cups
ounces salt » teaspoons	1-ounce salt	5 teaspoons
ounces jam » tablespoons	1-ounce jam	1.33 tablespoons
MASS TO WEIGHT		
ounce » pounds	1 ounce	0.0625 pounds
ounce » grams	1 ounce	28.35 grams
pounds » ounces	1 pound	16 ounces
pounds » kg	1 pound	0.45kg
kg » pounds	1 kg	2.2 pounds
grams » ounces	1 gram	0.035ounces
ENGLISH TO METRIC		
cup (U.S.) » mL	1 cup (U.S.)	236.58 mL
cup (U.K.) » mL	1 cup (U.K.)	284 mL
cup (Australia) » mL	1 cup (Australia)	250 mL
gallon (US) » L	1 gallon (US)	3.785 L
quart (US) » L	1 quart (US)	0.946 L
pint (US) » L	1 pint (US)	0.47 L
fluid ounces (US) » mL	1 fluid ounce (US)	29.57mL
tablespoons (US) » mL	1 tablespoon (US)	14.78 mL
teaspoons (US) » mL	1 teaspoon (US)	4.9285 mL
mL » cc	1 mL	1 cc

INDEX

O

P

Q

R

S

T

V

W

Dear reader, I hope you enjoyed my book. Here, you can find a detailed work-out section with all the exercises you can do at your home or at gym during low-carb and high-carb days.

Thank you for your purchase!

Printed in Great Britain
by Amazon